LIVING THE QUESTIONS IN Matthew

LIVING THE QUESTIONS IN Matthew

A NavStudy Featuring

NAVPRESS®

BRINGING TRUTH TO LIFE

OUR GUARANTEE TO YOU

We believe so strongly in the message of our books that we are making this quality guarantee to you. If for any reason you are disappointed with the content of this book, return the title page to us with your name and address and we will refund to you the list price of the book. To help us serve you better, please briefly describe why you were disappointed. Mail your refund request to: NavPress, P.O. Box 35002, Colorado Springs, CO 80935.

The Navigators is an international Christian organization. Our mission is to reach, disciple, and equip people to know Christ and to make Him known through successive generations. We envision multitudes of diverse people in the United States and every other nation who have a passionate love for Christ, live a lifestyle of sharing Christ's love, and multiply spiritual laborers among those without Christ.

NavPress is the publishing ministry of The Navigators. NavPress publications help believers learn biblical truth and apply what they learn to their lives and ministries. Our mission is to stimulate spiritual formation among our readers.

ISBN 1-57683-833-1

Cover design by Disciple Design
Cover photo by Gary Walpole
Creative Team: Steve Parolini, Arvid Wallen, Cara Iverson, Pat Reinheimer

Written and compiled by John Blase

Some of the anecdotal illustrations in this book are true to life and are included with the permission of the persons involved. All other illustrations are composites of real situations, and any resemblance to people living or dead is coincidental.

All Scripture quotations in this publication are taken from *THE MESSAGE* (MSG). Copyright © 1993, 1994, 1995, 1996, 2000, 2001, 2002. Used by permission of NavPress Publishing Group.

Printed in Canada

1 2 3 4 5 6 7 8 9 10 / 09 08 07 06 05

FOR A FREE CATALOG OF
NAVPRESS BOOKS & BIBLE STUDIES,
CALL 1-800-366-7788 (USA)
OR 1-800-839-4769 (CANADA)

CONTENTS

ABOUT THE
LIVING THE QUESTIONS
SERIES

> I want to beg you, as much as I can . . . to be patient toward
> all that is unsolved in your heart and try to love the questions
> themselves like locked rooms and like books that are written
> in a very foreign tongue. Do not now seek the answers, which
> cannot be given you because you would not be able to live
> them. . . . Live the questions now. Perhaps you will
> then gradually, without noticing it, live along some
> distant day into the answer.
>
> RAINER MARIA RILKE, *LETTERS TO A YOUNG POET*

Christians usually think about Jesus as the One with all the answers; the God-man with the evidence the verdict demands; a divine answer-man, sent down to earth to give us just what we need. And yes, he did give us just what we needed. Yet a careful reading of the Gospels shows that Jesus asked just as many questions as he gave outright answers. You would not have found a "The Bible says it, I believe it, and that settles it" bumper sticker on Jesus' backpack. It was more like, "This is God's Word. Stop and think about it, and let's talk about it."

However, the perception of Jesus as the divine answer-man appeals to a great many people. Life has questions, so you go to the Scriptures, look on the right page, find the answers, and everything's good. But while that works great for algebra class, it just doesn't seem to work well for this thing called *life*. Could the "divine answer-man" approach be too simplistic? Too one-dimensional for such a deep character as Jesus Christ? For one, it seems to leave you and me, the children of

God, out of the picture. We're not colaborers with God; we're just laborers.

Jesus went about doing good. Apparently part of this "good" was asking great questions—questions that would cause people to stop and pause and ponder the things they were living for and what might be worth dying for; questions not bound by a calendar but applicable to the ages; questions as poignant today as they were then.

The book you hold in your hand takes the approach of looking at the questions found in the Gospels—the questions Jesus asked. The questions are specific to the text of Eugene Peterson's *The Message*. I'm talking about questions such as, "All this time and money wasted on fashion—do you think it makes that much difference?" or "Who needs a doctor: the healthy or the sick?" Our temptation might be to respond quickly because we think we know the answers. But what if these questions must be lived? Lived out in dimensions such as friendship, family, and church? Lived out in locales such as homes, classrooms, and forests primeval? Lived by the flesh and blood whose main focus is the future, and lived by those who think mainly of the past? And what if living out these questions might lead us one day, gradually, without noticing it, into The Answer—the One who described himself as the way, truth, and life?

Live the questions now.

HOW TO USE THIS DISCUSSION GUIDE

1. This NavStudy is meant to be completed on your own *and* in a small group. You'll want to line up your study group ahead of time. A group of four to six is optimal—any bigger and one or more members will likely be shut out of discussions. Your small group can also be two. Each person will need his or her own copy of this book.

2. Lessons open with a Scripture passage intended to help you to prepare your heart and mind for the content that follows. Don't skip over this preparation time. Use it to reflect, slow down from a busy life, and transition into your study time.

3. *Read* the Scripture passages and other readings in each lesson. Let it all soak in. Re-read if necessary. There's no blue ribbon for finishing quickly. Make notes in the white space on the page. If you like journaling, think of this as a space to journal. If you don't like journaling, just think of it as space to "think out loud on paper."

4. *Think* about what you read. Respond to the questions we've provided. Always ask, "What does this mean?" and "Why does this matter?" about the readings. Compare different Bible translations for Scripture readings. Respond to the questions we've provided, and then discuss the questions when you're in your small group. Allow the experience of others to broaden your wisdom. You'll be stretched—called upon to evaluate what you've discovered and asked to make practical sense of it. In community, that stretching can often be painful and sometimes even embarrassing. But your willingness to be transparent—your openness to the possibility of personal growth—will reap great rewards.

5. *Pray* as you go through the entire session: before you read a word, in the middle of your thinking process, when you get stuck on a concept or passage, and as you approach the time when you'll explore

these passages and thoughts together in a small group. Pause when you need to ask God for inspiration or when you need to cry out in frustration. Compose a prayer prompted by what you've uncovered in the readings and your responses to the "Think" questions.

6. *Live.* (That's "live" as in "rhymes with give" as in "Give me something I can really use in my life.") This is a place to choose one thing you can do to live out the question posed in the lesson. Don't try to craft a plan that is lofty or unreachable. Choose something small, something doable. Then, in your small group, talk about this "one thing." Commit to following through on your idea, wrestle with what that means in practical terms, and call upon your group members to hold you accountable.

7. *Follow up.* Don't let the life application drift away without action. Be accountable to small-group members and refer to previous "Live" as in "rhymes with give" sections often. Take time at the beginning of each new study to review. See how you're doing.

SMALL-GROUP STUDY TIPS

After going through each week's study on your own, it's time to sit down with others and go deeper. Here are a few thoughts on how to make the most of your small-group discussion time.

Set ground rules. You don't need many. Here are two:

First, you'll want group members to make a commitment to the entire ten-week study. Significant personal growth happens when group members spend enough time together to really get to know each other. Hit-and-miss attendance can hinder this growth.

Second, agree together that everyone's story is important. Time is a valuable commodity, so if you have an hour to spend together, do your best to give each person ample time to express concerns, pass along insights, and generally feel like a participating member of the group. Small-group discussions are not monologues. However, a one-person-dominated discussion isn't always a bad thing. Not only is your role in a small group to explore and expand your own understanding, it's also to support one another. If someone truly needs more of the floor, give it to him or her. There will be times when the needs of the one outweigh the needs of the many. Use good judgment and allow extra space when needed. *Your* time might be next week.

Meet regularly. Choose a time and place, and stick to it. Consistency removes stress that could otherwise frustrate discussion and subsequent personal growth.

Follow the book outline. Each week, open your small-group time with prayer, and read aloud the reflective Scripture passage that opens the lesson. Then go through the study together, reading each section aloud and discussing it with your group members. Tell others what you wrote. Write down new insights gleaned from other group members. Wrestle the questions together. When you get to the "Pray" section, ask for volunteers willing to read aloud their written prayers. Finally, spend a few minutes talking together about each person's "one thing" and how to achieve that goal.

Talk openly. If you enter this study with shields up, you're probably not alone. And you're not a "bad person" for your hesitation to unpack your life in front of friends or strangers. Maybe you're skeptical about the value of revealing to others the deepest parts of who you are. Maybe you're simply too afraid of what might fall out of the suitcase. You don't have to go to a place where you're uncomfortable. If you want to sit and listen, offer a few thoughts, or even express a surface level of your own pain, go ahead. But don't neglect what brings you to this place—that longing for meaning. You can't ignore it away. Dip your feet in the water of brutally honest discussion, and you may choose to dive in. There is healing here.

Stay on task. Refrain from sharing material that falls into the "too much information" category. Don't spill unnecessary stuff. If structure isn't your group's strength, try a few minutes of general comments about the study, and then take each question one at a time and give everyone in the group a chance to respond.

LESSON 1

"If I make you light-bearers, you don't think I'm going to hide you under a bucket, do you?" (Matthew 5:15)

Before You Begin

Take some time to reflect and prepare your heart and mind for this study. Read the following Scripture passage. Soak up God's Word. There's no hurry. Then, when you're ready, turn the page and begin.

1 JOHN 4:16-18

God is love. When we take up permanent residence in a life of love, we live in God and God lives in us. This way, love has the run of the house, becomes at home and mature in us, so that we're free of worry on Judgment Day—our standing in the world is identical with Christ's. There is no room in love for fear. Well-formed love banishes fear. Since fear is crippling, a fearful life—fear of death, fear of judgment—is one not yet fully formed in love.

READ

Matthew 5:13-16

"Let me tell you why you are here. You're here to be salt-seasoning that brings out the God-flavors of this earth. If you lose your saltiness, how will people taste godliness? You've lost your usefulness and will end up in the garbage.

"Here's another way to put it: You're here to be light, bringing out the God-colors in the world. God is not a secret to be kept. We're going public with this, as public as a city on a hill. **If I make you light-bearers, you don't think I'm going to hide you under a bucket, do you?** I'm putting you on a light stand. Now that I've put you there on a hilltop, on a light stand—shine! Keep open house; be generous with your lives. By opening up to others, you'll prompt people to open up with God, this generous Father in heaven."

THINK "If I make you light-bearers, you don't think I'm going to hide you under a bucket, do you?"

- What is your immediate response to this question?
- Why do you think you responded in this way?
- As you were growing up, what did you hear/think were the reasons why you're on earth? Who or where did that come from?
- Has that belief changed over time? Now what do you believe about why you're here?
- Look again at what Jesus said. What, if any, differences and similarities are there between his words and yours?

READ

From *Man's Search for Meaning*, by Viktor Frankl[1]

The tender beginnings of a psychotherapy or psychohygiene were, when they were possible at all in the camp, either individual or collective in nature. The individual psychotherapeutic attempts were often a kind of "life-saving procedure." The efforts were usually concerned with the prevention of suicides. A very strict camp ruling forbade any efforts to save a man who attempted suicide. It was forbidden, for example, to cut down a man who was trying to hang himself. Therefore, it was all important to prevent these attempts from occurring.

I remember two cases of would-be suicide, which bore a striking similarity to each other. Both men had talked of their intentions to commit suicide. Both used the typical argument—they had nothing more to expect from life. In both cases it was a question of getting them to realize that life was still expecting something from them; something in the future was expected of them. We found, in fact, that for the one it was his child whom he adored and who was waiting for him in a foreign country. For the other it was a thing, not a person.

This man was a scientist and had written a series of books which still needed to be finished. His work could not be done by anyone else, any more than another person could ever take the place of the father in his child's affections.

This uniqueness and singleness which distinguishes each individual and gives a meaning to his existence has a bearing on creative work as much as it does on human love. When the impossibility of replacing a person is realized, it allows the responsibility which a man has for his existence and its continuance to appear in all its magnitude. A man who becomes conscious of the responsibility he bears toward a human being who affectionately waits for him, or to an unfinished work, will never be able to throw away his life. He knows the "why" for his existence, and will be able to bear almost any "how."

THINK   "If I make you light-bearers, you don't think I'm
            going to hide you under a bucket, do you?"

- What thoughts do Frankl's words stir in you?
- "In both cases it was a question of getting them to realize that life was still expecting something from them; something in the future was expected of them." What are some things that life might still be expecting of you?
- What are your thoughts about this in light of Jesus' question? Does the prospect of being a light-bearer imply something God is expecting of you? Explain.
- "When the impossibility of replacing a person is realized, it allows the responsibility which a man has for his existence and its continuance to appear in all its magnitude." Do you really believe it's impossible to replace you? Why or why not?

READ

From *A River Runs Through It*, by Norman Maclean[2]

One great thing about fly fishing is that after a while nothing exists of the world but thoughts about fly fishing. It is also interesting that thoughts about fishing are often carried on in dialogue form where Hope and Fear—or, many times, two Fears—try to outweigh each other.

One Fear looked down the shoreline and said to me (a third person distinct from the two Fears), "There is nothing but rocks for thirty yards, but don't get scared and try to land him before you get all the way down to the first sandbar."

The Second Fear said, "It's forty, not thirty, yards to the first sandbar and the weather has been warm and the fish's mouth will be soft and he will work off the hook if you try to fight him forty yards downriver. It's not good but it will be best to try and land him on a rock that is closer."

The First Fear said, "There is a big rock in the river that you will have to take him past before you land him, but, if you hold the line tight enough on him to keep him this side of the rock, you will probably lose him."

The Second Fear said, "But if you let him get on the far side of the rock, the line will get caught under it, and you will be sure to lose him."

That's how you know when you have thought too much—when you become a dialogue between *You'll probably lose* and *You're sure to lose*.

THINK   "If I make you light-bearers, you don't think I'm going to hide you under a bucket, do you?"

- "Thoughts about fishing are often carried on in dialogue form where Hope and Fear . . . try to outweigh each other." Does this sound anything at all like someone you know? Does it sound like you?

• When was the last time a "dialogue" between Hope and Fear took place for you? Be specific.

• "When you become a dialogue between *You'll probably lose* and *You're sure to lose*," Maclean says, "That's how you know when you have thought too much." Martin Luther King called it the "paralysis of analysis." Think about a moment when you "thought too much" or became paralyzed in your actions, speech, and so on. Looking back, what was that moment asking for from you?

• In what ways, if any, does the "paralysis of analysis" live in your response to Jesus' question?

READ

From *Alley Violinist*, by Robert Lax[3]

> if you were an alley violinist
> and they threw you money from
> three windows
>
> and the first note contained
> a nickel and said:
> when you play, we dance and
> sing, signed
> a very poor family
>
> and the second one contained
> a dime and said:
> I like your playing very much,
> signed
> a sick old lady
>
> and the last one contained
> a dollar and said:
> beat it,
>
> would you:
> stand there and play?
> beat it?
> walk away playing your fiddle?

THINK   "If I make you light-bearers, you don't think I'm
going to hide you under a bucket, do you?"

- If you were an alley violinist, how would you answer the question at the conclusion of the poem? Why?
- Have you ever let someone buy you off so you'd lay down your fiddle and leave? How did you feel when that happened? Looking back, what did it cost you?

• What do your answers to the poem and the previous question say about your willingness to be a light-bearer?

READ

Daniel 1:3-13

The king told Ashpenaz, head of the palace staff, to get some Israelites from the royal family and nobility—young men who were healthy and handsome, intelligent and well-educated, good prospects for leadership positions in the government, perfect specimens!—and indoctrinate them in the Babylonian language and the lore of magic and fortunetelling. The king then ordered that they be served from the same menu as the royal table—the best food, the finest wine. After three years of training they would be given positions in the king's court.

Four young men from Judah . . . were among those selected. The head of the palace staff gave them Babylonian names: Daniel was named Belteshazzar, Hananiah was named Shadrach, Mishael was named Meshach, Azariah was named Abednego.

But Daniel determined that he would not defile himself by eating the king's food or drinking his wine, so he asked the head of the palace staff to exempt him from the royal diet. The head of the palace staff, by God's grace, liked Daniel, but he warned him, "I'm afraid of what my master the king will do. He is the one who assigned this diet and if he sees that you are not as healthy as the rest, he'll have my head!"

But Daniel appealed to a steward who had been assigned by the head of the palace staff to be in charge of Daniel, Hananiah, Mishael, and Azariah: "Try us out for ten days on a simple diet of vegetables and water. Then compare us with the young men who eat from the royal menu. Make your decision on the basis of what you see."

THINK   "If I make you light-bearers, you don't think I'm going to hide you under a bucket, do you?"

- Do you think you would have been as bold as Daniel in a circumstance similar to this one? Why or why not?

- When in life do you tend to "hide yourself under a bucket"?
- What would it take to give you confidence to be a light-bearer in even difficult or challenging situations?

PRAY

Look back at the "Think" sections. Ruminate on your responses. Let them distill into a prayer, and then write that prayer below.

O Perfect Love . . .

The issue of prayer is not prayer; the issue of prayer is God.

Abraham Heschel

LIVE

"If I make you light-bearers, you don't think I'm going to hide you under a bucket, do you?"

The challenge now is to take this question further along—to live out this question. Think of one thing, *just one*, that you can personally do to wrestle with the question, inhabit the character of it, and live it in everyday life. In the following space, jot down your thoughts on this "one thing." Read the Scripture and quotes that follow for additional inspiration. During the coming week, pray about this "one thing," talk with a close friend about it, and learn to live the question.

One thing...

There is no room in love for fear. Well-formed love banishes fear. Since fear is crippling, a fearful life—fear of death, fear of judgment—is one not yet fully formed in love.

1 John 4:18

Playing small doesn't serve the world. There's nothing enlightened about shrinking so that other people won't feel insecure around you. We were born to make manifest the glory of God that is within us. . . . And, as we let our own light shine, we unconsciously give other people permission to do the same. As we are liberated from our own fear, our presence automatically liberates others.

Nelson Mandela

Live the questions now. Perhaps you will then gradually, without noticing it, live along some distant day into the answer.

RAINER MARIA RILKE, *LETTERS TO A YOUNG POET*

"'Eye for eye, tooth for tooth.' Is that going to
get us anywhere?" (Matthew 5:38-39)

Before You Begin

Take some time to reflect and prepare your heart and
mind for this study. Read the following Scripture passage.
Soak up God's Word. There's no hurry. Then, when
you're ready, turn the page and begin.

Matthew 6:12-13

"Keep us forgiven with you and forgiving others.
Keep us safe from ourselves and the Devil.
You're in charge!
You can do anything you want!
You're ablaze in beauty!
      Yes. Yes. Yes."

READ

Matthew 5:38-45

"Here's another old saying that deserves a second look: '**Eye for eye, tooth for tooth.' Is that going to get us anywhere?** Here's what I propose: 'Don't hit back at all.' If someone strikes you, stand there and take it. If someone drags you into court and sues for the shirt off your back, giftwrap your best coat and make a present of it. And if someone takes unfair advantage of you, use the occasion to practice the servant life. No more tit-for-tat stuff. Live generously.

"You're familiar with the old written law, 'Love your friend,' and its unwritten companion, 'Hate your enemy.' I'm challenging that. I'm telling you to love your enemies. Let them bring out the best in you, not the worst. When someone gives you a hard time, respond with the energies of prayer, for then you are working out of your true selves, your God-created selves. This is what God does. He gives his best—the sun to warm and the rain to nourish—to everyone, regardless: the good and bad, the nice and nasty."

THINK   "'Eye for eye, tooth for tooth.' Is that going to get us anywhere?"

- What is your immediate response to this question?
- Why do you think you responded in this way?
- Think through your gut-level reaction to the statement, "If someone strikes you, stand there and take it." When was the last time you stood there and took it? Be specific here—names, places, details.
- Did it get you anywhere? How have you handled it since then?
- Were you proud of yourself in that moment, or . . . ?

THINK (continued)

READ

From *To Kill a Mockingbird*, by Harper Lee[1]

According to Miss Stephanie Crawford . . . Atticus was leaving the post office when Mr. Ewell approached him, cursed him, spat on him, and threatened to kill him. Miss Stephanie (who, by the time she had told it twice was there and had seen it all — passing by from the Jitney Jungle, she was) — Miss Stephanie said Atticus didn't bat an eye, just took out his handkerchief and wiped his face and stood there and let Mr. Ewell call him names wild horses could not bring her to repeat. Mr. Ewell was a veteran of an obscure war, that plus Atticus's peaceful reaction probably prompted him to inquire, "Too proud to fight?" . . . Miss Stephanie said Atticus said, "No, too old," put his hands in his pockets and strolled on. Miss Stephanie said you had to hand it to Atticus Finch, he could be right dry sometimes.

"Jem, see if you can stand in Bob Ewell's shoes a minute. I destroyed his last shred of credibility at that trial, if he had any to begin with. The man had to have some kind of a comeback. . . . So if spitting in my face and threatening me saved Mayella Ewell one extra beating, that's something I'll gladly take. He had to take it out on somebody and I'd rather it be me than that houseful of children out there. You understand?"

THINK   "'Eye for eye, tooth for tooth.' Is that going to get us anywhere?"

- Do you think you could have done what Atticus did, or is that kind of behavior only for saints?
- Atticus asked Jem if she understood. Do *you*? What do you hear him saying about the situation?
- Do you think Atticus might have fought back in his younger days?
- What's your take on Atticus's behavior? Is this true strength, or glorified passivity?

THINK (continued)

READ

From *A Fable*, by Louise Gluck[2]

Two women with
the same claim
came to the feet of
the wise king. Two women,
but only one baby.
The king knew
someone was lying.
What he said was
Let the child be
cut in half; that way
no one will go
empty-handed. He
drew his sword.
Then, of the two
women, one
renounced her share:
this was the sign, the lesson.
Suppose
you saw your mother
torn between two daughters:
what could you do
to save her but be
willing to destroy
yourself—she would know
who was the rightful child,
the one who couldn't bear
to divide the mother.

THINK   "'Eye for eye, tooth for tooth.' Is that going to get us anywhere?"

- Most of our enemies aren't miles away; they're frighteningly close by. Are you and a family member or close friend standing at "the feet of the wise king" making "the same claim"?
- What is the "baby" you're fighting over?
- Has either one of you been willing to renounce your share? Why or why not?

READ

From *Traveling Mercies*, by Anne Lamott[3]

I'd had an enemy—an Enemy Lite—for some time, the parent of one of the children in Sam's first grade class, although she was so warm and friendly that it might have astounded her to learn that we were enemies. . . . There were all these mothers who were always cooking holiday theme-park treats for the class; they always drove the kids—including mine—on their field trips, and they also seemed to read all the papers the school sent home, which I think is actually a little show-offy. Also, it gave them an unfair advantage. They knew, for instance, from the first day of school that Wednesdays were minimum days, with school out over forty-five minutes earlier than usual, and they flaunted it, picking up their kids at just the right time, week after week. I somehow managed to make it into October without figuring out this little scheduling quirk.

Finally, though, one Wednesday, I stopped by Sam's classroom and found him—once again—drawing with his teacher. The teacher said gently, "Annie? Did you not know that school gets out early on Wednesdays?"

"Ah," I said. . . .

Well, my enemy found out.

She showed up two days later all bundled up in a down jacket, because it was cold and she was one of the parents who was driving kids on their first field trip. Now, this was not a crime against nature or me in and of itself. The crime was that below that down jacket, she was wearing latex bicycle shorts. She wears latex bicycle shorts nearly every day, and I will tell you why: because she can. She weighs almost eighty pounds. She has gone to the gym almost every day since her divorce, and she does not have an ounce of fat on her body. I completely hate that in a person. . . .

The day of the field trip, she said sweetly, "I just want you to know, Annie, that if you have any other questions about how the classroom works, I'd really love to be there for you."

I smiled back at her: I thought such awful thoughts that I

cannot even say them out loud because they would make Jesus want to drink gin straight out of the cat dish.

It drove me to my knees. I prayed about it. I prayed because my son loves her son, and my son is so kind that it makes me want to be a better person, a person who does not hate someone just because she wears latex bicycle shorts. I prayed for a miracle; I wrote her name down on a slip of paper, folded it up, and put it in the box that I use as God's In box. "Help," I said to God. . . .

And I finally got it.

The veil dropped. I got that I am as mad as a hatter. I saw that *I* was the one worried that my child wasn't doing well enough in school. That *I* was the one who thought I was out of shape. And that I was trying to get her to carry all this for me because it hurt too much to carry it myself.

I wanted to kiss her on both cheeks, apologize for all the self-contempt I'd been spewing out into the world, all the bad juju I'd been putting on her by thinking she was the one doing harm.

THINK   "'Eye for eye, tooth for tooth.' Is that going to get us anywhere?"

- What is your first reaction to Lamott's mini-drama?
- Is there anything in her words that you can identify with?
- Is prayer a first response when you're confronted with enemies, be they Lite or Heavy? Why or why not?
- How do you respond to secret enemies (enemies who don't know you consider them as such) such as the one Lamott describes? How does Jesus' question play into this kind of situation?

READ

Genesis 27:1-27,30-41; 33:1-11

When Isaac had become an old man and was nearly blind, he called his eldest son, Esau, and said, "My son."

"Yes, Father?"

"I'm an old man," he said; "I might die any day now. Do me a favor: Get your quiver of arrows and your bow and go out in the country and hunt me some game. Then fix me a hearty meal, the kind that you know I like, and bring it to me to eat so that I can give you my personal blessing before I die."

Rebekah was eavesdropping as Isaac spoke to his son Esau. As soon as Esau had gone off to the country to hunt game for his father, Rebekah spoke to her son Jacob. "I just overheard your father talking with your brother, Esau. He said, 'Bring me some game and fix me a hearty meal so that I can eat and bless you with GOD's blessing before I die.'

"Now, my son, listen to me. Do what I tell you. Go to the flock and get me two young goats. Pick the best; I'll prepare them into a hearty meal, the kind that your father loves. Then you'll take it to your father, he'll eat and bless you before he dies."

"But Mother," Jacob said, "my brother Esau is a hairy man and I have smooth skin. What happens if my father touches me? He'll think I'm playing games with him. I'll bring down a curse on myself instead of a blessing."

"If it comes to that," said his mother, "I'll take the curse on myself. Now, just do what I say. Go and get the goats."

So he went and got them and brought them to his mother and she cooked a hearty meal, the kind his father loved so much.

Rebekah took the dress-up clothes of her older son Esau and put them on her younger son Jacob. She took the goatskins and covered his hands and the smooth nape of his neck. Then she placed the hearty meal she had fixed and fresh bread she'd baked into the hands of her son Jacob.

He went to his father and said, "My father!"

"Yes?" he said. "Which son are you?"

Jacob answered his father, "I'm your firstborn son Esau. I did what you told me. Come now; sit up and eat of my game so you can give me your personal blessing."

Isaac said, "So soon? How did you get it so quickly?"

"Because your GOD cleared the way for me."

Isaac said, "Come close, son; let me touch you—are you really my son Esau?"

So Jacob moved close to his father Isaac. Isaac felt him and said, "The voice is Jacob's voice but the hands are the hands of Esau." He didn't recognize him because his hands were hairy, like his brother Esau's.

But as he was about to bless him he pressed him, "You're sure? *You* are my son Esau?"

"Yes. I am."

Isaac said, "Bring the food so I can eat of my son's game and give you my personal blessing." Jacob brought it to him and he ate. He also brought him wine and he drank.

Then Isaac said, "Come close, son, and kiss me."

He came close and kissed him and Isaac smelled the smell of his clothes. Finally, he blessed him. . . .

And then right after Isaac had blessed Jacob and Jacob had left, Esau showed up from the hunt. He also had prepared a hearty meal. He came to his father and said, "Let my father get up and eat of his son's game, that he may give me his personal blessing."

His father Isaac said, "And who are you?"

"I am your son, your firstborn, Esau."

Isaac started to tremble, shaking violently. He said, "Then who hunted game and brought it to me? I finished the meal just now, before you walked in. And I blessed him—he's blessed for good!"

Esau, hearing his father's words, sobbed violently and most bitterly, and cried to his father, "My father! Can't you also bless me?"

Your brother," he said, "came here falsely and took your blessing."

Esau said, "Not for nothing was he named Jacob, the Heel.

Twice now he's tricked me: first he took my birthright and now he's taken my blessing."

He begged, "Haven't you kept back any blessing for me?"

Isaac answered Esau, "I've made him your master, and all his brothers his servants, and lavished grain and wine on him. I've given it all away. What's left for you, my son?"

"But don't you have just one blessing for me, Father? Oh, bless me my father! Bless me!" Esau sobbed inconsolably.

Isaac said to him,

> You'll live far from Earth's bounty,
>   remote from Heaven's dew.
> You'll live by your sword, hand-to-mouth,
>   and you'll serve your brother.
> But when you can't take it any more
>   you'll break loose and run free.

Esau seethed in anger against Jacob because of the blessing his father had given him; he brooded, "The time for mourning my father's death is close. And then I'll kill my brother Jacob." . . .

Jacob looked up and saw Esau coming with his four hundred men. He divided the children between Leah and Rachel and the two maidservants. He put the maidservants out in front, Leah and her children next, and Rachel and Joseph last. He led the way and, as he approached his brother, bowed seven times, honoring his brother. But Esau ran up and embraced him, held him tight and kissed him. And they both wept.

Then Esau looked around and saw the women and children: "And who are these with you?"

Jacob said, "The children that God saw fit to bless me with."

Then the maidservants came up with their children and bowed; then Leah and her children, also bowing; and finally, Joseph and Rachel came up and bowed to Esau.

Esau then asked, "And what was the meaning of all those herds that I met?"

"I was hoping that they would pave the way for my master to welcome me."

Esau said, "Oh, brother. I have plenty of everything—keep what is yours for yourself."

Jacob said, "Please. If you can find it in your heart to welcome me, accept these gifts. When I saw your face, it was as the face of God smiling on me." . . . Jacob urged the gifts on him and Esau accepted.

THINK

"'Eye for eye, tooth for tooth.' Is that going to get us anywhere?"

- Esau had every right to be upset with Jacob. How does his response match up with Jesus' question?
- Here in this Old Testament story, there is a picture of forgiveness that shatters the status quo. In what ways did Esau's response to Jacob help them to "get somewhere" in their relationship?
- Think about your relationships that have been damaged or are strained. Has "eye for eye" worked for you? Why or why not?
- What do you need to do to get somewhere in those relationships?

PRAY

Look back at the "Think" sections. Ruminate on your responses.
Let them distill into a prayer, and then write that prayer below.

O Wise King . . .

The issue of prayer is not prayer; the issue of prayer is God.
ABRAHAM HESCHEL

LIVE   "'Eye for eye, tooth for tooth.' Is that going to get us anywhere?"

The challenge now is to take this question further along—to live out this question. Think of one thing, *just one*, that you can personally do to wrestle with the question, inhabit the character of it, and live it in everyday life. In the following space, jot down your thoughts on this "one thing." Read the Scripture and quotes that follow for additional inspiration. During the coming week, pray about this "one thing," talk with a close friend about it, and learn to live the question.

One thing...

> Post this at all the intersections, dear friends: Lead with your ears, follow up with your tongue, and let anger straggle along in the rear. God's righteousness doesn't grow from human anger.
>
> James 1:19-20
>
> One of the most time-consuming things is to have an enemy.
> E. B. White

Live the questions now. Perhaps you will then gradually, without noticing it, live along some distant day into the answer.
RAINER MARIA RILKE, *LETTERS TO A YOUNG POET*

"All this time and money wasted on fashion — do you think it makes that much difference?" (Matthew 6:28)

Before You Begin

Take some time to reflect and prepare your heart and mind for this study. Read the following Scripture passage. Soak up God's Word. There's no hurry. Then, when you're ready, turn the page and begin.

Psalm 46:10

"Step out of the traffic! Take a long,
  loving look at me, your High God."

READ

Matthew 6:25-33

"If you decide for God, living a life of God-worship, it follows that you don't fuss about what's on the table at mealtimes or whether the clothes in your closet are in fashion. There is far more to your life than the food you put in your stomach, more to your outer appearance than the clothes you hang on your body. Look at the birds, free and unfettered, not tied down to a job description, careless in the care of God. And you count far more to him than birds.

"Has anyone by fussing in front of the mirror ever gotten taller by so much as an inch? **All this time and money wasted on fashion—do you think it makes that much difference?** Instead of looking at the fashions, walk out into the fields and look at the wildflowers. They never primp or shop, but have you ever seen color and design quite like it? The ten best-dressed men and women in the country look shabby alongside them.

"If God gives such attention to the appearance of wild-flowers—most of which are never even seen—don't you think he'll attend to you, take pride in you, do his best for you? What I'm trying to do here is to get you to relax, to not be so preoccupied with *getting*, so you can respond to God's *giving*. People who don't know God and the way he works fuss over these things, but you know both God and how he works. Steep your life in God-reality, God-initiative, God-provisions. Don't worry about missing out. You'll find all your everyday human concerns will be met."

THINK   "All this time and money wasted on fashion— do you think it makes that much difference?"

• What is your immediate response to this question?
• Why do you think you responded in this way?

- Think about the number of clothing catalogs you've received in the last six months or about the number of food commercials you see during any given sitcom. Have you ever considered these things enemy fire?
- Jesus is talking about more than khakis and fettuccine here. What do you hear him saying?

READ

From *The Age of Innocence*, by Edith Wharton[1]

In the middle of the room she paused, looking about her with a grave mouth and smiling eyes; and in that instant Newland Archer rejected the general verdict on her looks. It was true that her early radiance was gone. The red cheeks had paled; she was thin, worn, a little older-looking than her age, which must have been nearly thirty. But there was about her the mysterious authority of beauty, a sureness in the carriage of the head, the movement of the eyes, which, without being in the least theatrical, struck him as highly trained and full of a conscious power. At the same time she was simpler in nature than most of the ladies present, and many people (as he heard afterward from Janey) were disappointed that her appearance was not more "stylish"—for stylishness was what New York most valued. It was, perhaps, Archer reflected, because her early vivacity had disappeared; because she was so quiet—quiet in her movements, her voice, and the tones of her low-pitched voice. New York had expected something a good deal more resonant in a young woman with such a history.

THINK "All this time and money wasted on fashion — do you think it makes that much difference?"

- Have you ever felt that someone was "disappointed" in you because you were not more stylish? (Don't limit the question or your answer to clothing.)
- How long ago was this, and how did you handle the situation?
- Note that the statement "for stylishness was what New York most valued" was written in 1920. (Some things never change!) What things do the people in your circle value most? How do you deal with that?

- Countess Olenska (described in the passage) has what Wharton calls a "mysterious authority of beauty, a sureness . . . highly trained and full of a conscious power." Male or female, would you be willing to trade what's in your closet for that?

READ

From *Celebration of Discipline*, by Richard Foster [2]

Because we lack a divine Center our need for security has led us into an insane attachment to things. We really must understand that the lust for affluence in contemporary society is psychotic. It is psychotic because it has completely lost touch with reality. We crave things we neither need nor enjoy. "We buy things we do not want to impress people we do not like." [3] Where planned obsolescence leaves off, psychological obsolescence takes over. We are made to feel ashamed to wear clothes or drive cars until they are worn out. The mass media have convinced us that to be out of step with fashion is to be out of step with reality. It is time we awaken to the fact that conformity to a sick society is to be sick.

THINK   "All this time and money wasted on fashion — do you think it makes that much difference?"

- Have you ever bought something you didn't want in order to impress someone you didn't like?
- "We are made to feel ashamed to wear clothes or drive cars until they are worn out." How do you view people who wear or drive things until they are worn out?
- "It is time we awaken to the fact that conformity to a sick society is to be sick." Is it time for you to wake up? What would that look like?
- And just what are you waking up to?

READ

From *A Traveler Toward the Dawn*, by John Eagan[4]

The next day I biked against a strong north wind in the glory of a cold front and came to my "sacred spot," a farmer's lonely meadow, surrounded by forest, with a stream flowing through it; there in the meadow I lifted my face to the God of creation and reverenced him. I adored him, Father and Son and Holy Spirit. Then I lay before him face down in prayer as a beggar and a sinner asking for all my needs; then I lay on my back open to the sun, asking him for the greatest possible openness of spirit, giving myself to him as I am and being quiet in that self-surrender. I felt very at home in the middle of nature under the open sky. There were breathtaking moments when the wind, the breath of creation, blew and rippled the long grass and the whole of nature seemed to vibrate with God present. And I was part of this universe, one with it.

After a while I opened Luke's Gospel to chapter twelve and asked the Holy Spirit to open Scripture to me and speak through that word. Suddenly there it was: his living word coming strong into my mind and heart and filling me. How striking it was to walk in the grass barefoot . . . and to hear the Lord say: "Why worry about your clothing, what to put on or what to eat?" Overhead an eagle or big hawk soared, effortlessly playing off the wind. "Look at the birds of the air, God takes care of them." I walked through lovely yellow spring flowers sprinkling that meadow, splendid in their glory. "God takes care of all of them; how much more will he take care of you?" . . .

For an hour and a half I stayed there, feeling so much at home with my Lord, endlessly nourished by Luke's words. Then I rode back to the retreat house with a settled peace and quiet enveloping me. Twice I went into the chapel and came close to Jesus and asked him to draw me to himself. I felt love flaming out and hunger and thirst for him growing. That whole evening was so calm and peaceful and healthy. I felt healthier than ever before and poised and sure in the Lord. And all this without effort, just

being with God and experiencing little rivers of joy and desire
suddenly starting in me.

From *A Timbered Choir*, by Wendell Berry[5]

I go among the trees and sit still.
All my stirring becomes quiet
around me like circles on water.
My tasks lie in their places
where I left them, asleep like cattle.

Then what is afraid of me comes
and lives for a while in my sight.
What it fears in me leaves me,
and the fear of me leaves it.
It sings, and I hear its song.

Then what I am afraid of comes.
I live for a while in its sight.
What I fear in it leaves it,
and the fear of it leaves me.
It sings, and I hear its song.

After days of labor,
mute in my consternations,
I hear my song at last,
and I sing it. As we sing,
the day turns, the trees move.

THINK   "All this time and money wasted on fashion —
do you think it makes that much difference?"

• Jesus specifically mentions wildflowers and birds. Eagan experi-
ences God's care while on his back in a meadow. Berry has all
his "stirring" stilled among the trees. What is your reaction to
these nature-sounding readings?

• How far removed is your life from the birds of the air, wild-flowers in the meadow, and trees in the forest? What role, if any, does "time and money wasted on fashion" play in your answer to this question?

• If God's creation doesn't play a regular role in your devotional life, what can you do to change that? (This means more than an annual trip to the woods.)

READ

Genesis 1:26-31

> God spoke: "Let us make human beings in our image, make
> > them
> > reflecting our nature
> So they can be responsible for the fish in the sea,
> > the birds in the air, the cattle,
> And, yes, Earth itself,
> > and every animal that moves on the face of Earth."
> God created human beings;
> > he created them godlike,
> Reflecting God's nature.
> > He created them male and female.
> God blessed them:
> > "Prosper! Reproduce! Fill Earth! Take charge!
> Be responsible for fish in the sea and birds in the air,
> > for every living thing that moves on the face of Earth."

> Then God said, "I've given you
> > every sort of seed-bearing plant on Earth
> And every kind of fruit-bearing tree,
> > given them to you for food.
> To all animals and all birds,
> > everything that moves and breathes,
> I give whatever grows out of the ground for food."
> > And there it was

> God looked over everything he had made;
> > it was so good, so very good!

THINK   "All this time and money wasted on fashion —
             do you think it makes that much difference?"

- What, if anything, does this Creation passage tell you about the quest for fashion?
- How does this passage influence your response to Jesus' question?
- Is this a different answer than you used to have? What changed?

PRAY

Look back at the "Think" sections. Ruminate on your responses. Let them distill into a prayer, and then write that prayer below.

Lord of all creation . . .

The issue of prayer is not prayer; the issue of prayer is God.

ABRAHAM HESCHEL

LIVE   "All this time and money wasted on fashion — do you think it makes that much difference?"

The challenge now is to take this question further along — to live out this question. Think of one thing, *just one*, that you can personally do to wrestle with the question, inhabit the character of it, and live it in everyday life. In the following space, jot down your thoughts on this "one thing." Read the Scripture and quotes that follow for additional inspiration. During the coming week, pray about this "one thing," talk with a close friend about it, and learn to live the question.

One thing . . .

"Look at the birds, free and unfettered. . . . Instead of looking at the fashions . . . look at the wildflowers."

Matthew 6:26,28

God's glory is on tour in the skies,
    God-craft on exhibit across the horizon.
Madame Day holds classes every morning,
    Professor Night lectures each evening.

Their words aren't heard,
    their voices aren't recorded,
But their silence fills the earth:
    unspoken truth is spoken everywhere.

Psalm 19:1-4

Live the questions now. Perhaps you will then gradually, without noticing it, live along some distant day into the answer.

RAINER MARIA RILKE, *LETTERS TO A YOUNG POET*

"Who needs a doctor: the healthy or the sick?"
(Matthew 9:12)

Before You Begin

Take some time to reflect and prepare your heart and mind for this study. Read the following Scripture passage. Soak up God's Word. There's no hurry. Then, when you're ready, turn the page and begin.

Matthew 19:14

But Jesus intervened: "Let the children alone, don't prevent them from coming to me. God's kingdom is made up of people like these."

READ

Matthew 9:1-13

Back in the boat, Jesus and the disciples recrossed the sea to Jesus' hometown. They were hardly out of the boat when some men carried a paraplegic on a stretcher and set him down in front of them. Jesus, impressed by their bold belief, said to the paraplegic, "Cheer up, son. I forgive your sins." Some religion scholars whispered, "Why, that's blasphemy!"

Jesus knew what they were thinking, and said, "Why this gossipy whispering? Which do you think is simpler: to say, 'I forgive your sins,' or, 'Get up and walk'? Well, just so it's clear that I'm the Son of Man and authorized to do either, or both. . . ." At this he turned to the paraplegic and said, "Get up. Take your bed and go home." And the man did it. The crowd was awestruck, amazed and pleased that God had authorized Jesus to work among them this way.

Passing along, Jesus saw a man at his work collecting taxes. His name was Matthew. Jesus said, "Come along with me." Matthew stood up and followed him.

Later when Jesus was eating supper at Matthew's house with his close followers, a lot of disreputable characters came and joined them. When the Pharisees saw him keeping this kind of company, they had a fit, and lit into Jesus' followers. "What kind of example is this from your Teacher, acting cozy with crooks and riff-raff?"

Jesus, overhearing, shot back, "**Who needs a doctor: the healthy or the sick?** Go figure out what this Scripture means: 'I'm after mercy, not religion.' I'm here to invite outsiders, not coddle insiders."

THINK   "Who needs a doctor: the healthy or the sick?"

• What is your immediate response to this question?
• Why do you think you responded in this way?

- When was the last time you spent significant time with a paraplegic, an IRS agent, a known felon, or the locals that most people hope their sons and daughters do *not* marry?
- "You are known by the company you keep." What memories or emotions does this phrase evoke?
- What do you think Jesus means by "I'm after mercy, not religion"?

READ

From *Messy Spirituality*, by Michael Yaconelli[1]

When Jesus and his followers show up, it isn't long before people start pointing fingers and calling names. Jesus was called all kinds of names: wine-bibber (what is a wine-bibber, anyway?), Sabbath breaker, blasphemer. Over the centuries, religious people have refined name calling to an art. . . . According to his critics, Jesus "did God" all wrong. He went to the wrong places, said the wrong things, and worst of all, let just anyone into the kingdom. Jesus scandalized an intimidating, elitist, country-club religion by opening membership in the spiritual life to those who had been denied it. What made people furious was Jesus' "irresponsible" habit of throwing open the doors of his love to the whosoevers, the just-any-ones, and the not-a-chancers like you and me.

Nothing makes people in the church more angry than grace. It's ironic: we stumble into a party we weren't invited to and find the uninvited standing at the door making sure no other uninviteds get in. Then a strange phenomenon occurs: as soon as we are included in the party because of Jesus' irresponsible love, we decide to make grace "more responsible" by becoming self-appointed Kingdom Monitors, guarding the kingdom of God, keeping the riffraff out (which, as I understand it, are who the kingdom of God is supposed to include).

THINK   "Who needs a doctor: the healthy or the sick?"

- Can you recall a time when your experience of God's people was like an "intimidating, elitist, country-club religion"?
- As you think about that time, were there some "irresponsible" people in that group—people who just kept letting the riffraff in? How did that make you feel? How do you think it made others feel?

- Yaconelli says, "Nothing makes people in the church more angry than grace." What is your response to that? If grace makes you angry, why?

READ

From *The Return of the Prodigal Son*, by Henri Nouwen[2]

The lostness of the elder son . . . is much harder to identify. After all, he did all the right things. He was obedient, dutiful, law-abiding, and hardworking. People respected him, admired him, praised him, and likely considered him a model son. Outwardly, the elder son was faultless. But when confronted by his father's joy at the return of his younger brother, a dark power erupts in him and boils to the surface. Suddenly, there becomes glaringly visible a resentful, proud, unkind, selfish person, one that had remained deeply hidden, even though it had been growing stronger and more powerful over the years.

Looking deeply into myself and then around me at the lives of other people, I wonder which does more damage, lust or resentment? There is so much resentment among the "just" and the "righteous." There is so much judgment, condemnation, and prejudice among the "saints." There is so much frozen anger among the people who are so concerned about avoiding "sin."

The lostness of the resentful "saint" is so hard to reach precisely because it is so closely wedded to the desire to be good and virtuous. I know, from my own life, how diligently I have tried to be good, acceptable, likable, and a worthy example for others. There was always the conscious effort to avoid the pitfalls of sin and the constant fear of giving in to temptation. But with all of that there came a seriousness, a moralistic intensity—and even a touch of fanaticism—that made it increasingly difficult to feel at home in my Father's house.

THINK "Who needs a doctor: the healthy or the sick?"

- Did anything "speak" to you as you read Nouwen's words? If so, what?
- What do you think does more damage: lust or resentment? Why do you think that?

- Would people describe you as serious, morally intense, maybe even fanatical? Would you consider yourself "healthy" or "sick" because of that?
- It's common to think of Jesus' question as one of how we consider others, but what does it say to you about you?
- Do you feel "at home" in God's household? What does that say about the manner in which you view Jesus' question about who needs a doctor?

READ

From *The Last Bus to Albuquerque*, by Lewis Grizzard[3]

Whenever I left my late mother's home, and we are talking a period of over forty years, she would always end her goodbyes with these two words: "Be sweet."

When I was a child on my way to a friend's birthday party, I suppose that meant not to stick my finger in the cake or do a lot of whining and crying.

In my teen years it meant not to steal any hubcaps.

As an adult, I guess now she was beseeching me not to rob a liquor store, engage in any insider trading, and to go out amongst them each day with a smile and agreeable disposition.

I can't recall sticking my finger into too many birthday cakes, but I very likely ignored the part about no whining nor crying when things didn't go my way on occasion—such as when I pinned the tail on the donkey's esophagus.

I never stole a hubcap. Not one.

As an adult I've never robbed anything nor have I engaged in much of any kind of trading that was profitable.

But the other stuff—the daily smile, the agreeable disposition—well, I've had my failures.

I notoriously have not been sweet to such individuals as waiters and waitresses I've deemed slow or unable to service correctly what I considered to be the simplest of orders.

Many a rental car clerk has known my verbal wrath, not to mention motel housekeepers who bang on my door too quickly after the first crow of morning, people I don't know who address me as "buddy" and liberals.

Yet, my mother's words, so simple, were so implicit: Be sweet.

THINK   "Who needs a doctor: the healthy or the sick?"

- What words like Grizzard's "Be sweet" did you hear from parents or other authority figures while you were growing up? How did you respond to those words?
- We're back where we started (see first "Read" section in this lesson). *Now* what do you think Jesus means by "I'm after mercy, not religion"?
- How do you feel now about making clear distinctions between who's "healthy" and who's "sick"? Which are you?
- What if all the books on Christian discipleship, ethics, community, and so on were condensed into two words and we discovered that Jesus just wanted us to "be sweet"? Sound too simplistic? Why?

READ

Deuteronomy 6:3-9

Listen obediently, Israel. Do what you're told so that you'll have a good life, a life of abundance and bounty, just as GOD promised, in a land abounding in milk and honey.

Attention, Israel!

GOD, our God! GOD the one and only!

Love GOD, your God, with your whole heart: love him with all that's in you, love him with all you've got!

Write these commandments that I've given you today on your hearts. Get them inside of you and then get them inside your children. Talk about them wherever you are, sitting at home or walking in the street; talk about them from the time you get up in the morning to when you fall into bed at night. Tie them on your hands and foreheads as a reminder; inscribe them on the doorposts of your homes and on your city gates.

Matthew 22:36-40

"Teacher, which command in God's Law is the most important?"

Jesus said, "'Love the Lord your God with all your passion and prayer and intelligence.' This is the most important, the first on any list. But there is a second to set alongside it: 'Love others as well as you love yourself.' These two commands are pegs; everything in God's Law and the Prophets hangs from them."

THINK   *"Who needs a doctor: the healthy or the sick?"*

- What does it mean to "write these commandments . . . on your hearts"? How do you do that?
- In what ways do the Ten Commandments speak to Jesus' question about who needs a doctor (see Deuteronomy 5)?

- How does loving God with your whole heart—with your "passion and prayer and intelligence"—impact the way you respond to others around you?
- How does loving "others as well as you love yourself" impact the way in which you answer Jesus' question? Who are the "others" you have a hard time loving? What would it take to change that?

PRAY

Look back at the "Think" sections. Ruminate on your responses.
Let them distill into a prayer, and then write that prayer below.

Merciful Father . . .

The issue of prayer is not prayer; the issue of prayer is God.

ABRAHAM HESCHEL

LIVE

"Who needs a doctor: the healthy or the sick?"

The challenge now is to take this question further along—to live out this question. Think of one thing, *just one*, that you can personally do to wrestle with the question, inhabit the character of it, and live it in everyday life. In the following space, jot down your thoughts on this "one thing." Read the Scripture and quotes that follow for additional inspiration. During the coming week, pray about this "one thing," talk with a close friend about it, and learn to live the question.

One thing . . .

"The next time you put on a dinner, don't just invite your friends and family and rich neighbors, the kind of people who will return the favor. Invite some people who never get invited out, the misfits from the wrong side of the tracks. You'll be—and experience—a blessing."

Luke 14:12-14

"I'm after mercy, not religion."

Matthew 9:13

Live the questions now. Perhaps you will then gradually, without noticing it, live along some distant day into the answer.
RAINER MARIA RILKE, *LETTERS TO A YOUNG POET*

LESSON 5

"If they call me, the Master, 'Dungface,' what can the workers expect?" (Matthew 10:25)

Before You Begin

Take some time to reflect and prepare your heart and mind for this study. Read the following Scripture passage. Soak up God's Word. There's no hurry. Then, when you're ready, turn the page and begin.

JOHN 16:1-3

"I've told you these things to prepare you for rough times ahead. They are going to throw you out of the meeting places. There will even come a time when anyone who kills you will think he's doing God a favor. They will do these things because they never really understood the Father."

READ

Matthew 10:16-28

"Stay alert. This is hazardous work I'm assigning you. You're going to be like sheep running through a wolf pack, so don't call attention to yourselves. Be as cunning as a snake, inoffensive as a dove.

"Don't be naive. Some people will impugn your motives, others will smear your reputation—just because you believe in me. Don't be upset when they haul you before the civil authorities. Without knowing it, they've done you—and me—a favor, given you a platform for preaching the kingdom news! And don't worry about what you'll say or how you'll say it. The right words will be there; the Spirit of your Father will supply the words.

"When people realize it is the living God you are presenting and not some idol that makes them feel good, they are going to turn on you, even people in your own family. There is a great irony here: proclaiming so much love, experiencing so much hate! But don't quit. Don't cave in. It is all well worth it in the end. It is not success you are after in such times but survival. Be survivors! Before you've run out of options, the Son of Man will have arrived.

"A student doesn't get a better desk than her teacher. A laborer doesn't make more money than his boss. Be content—pleased, even—when you, my students, my harvest hands, get the same treatment I get. **If they call me, the Master, 'Dungface,' what can the workers expect?**

"Don't be intimidated. Eventually everything is going to be out in the open, and everyone will know how things really are. So don't hesitate to go public now.

"Don't be bluffed into silence by the threats of bullies. There's nothing they can do to your soul, your core being. Save your fear for God, who holds your entire life—body and soul—in his hands."

THINK   "If they call me, the Master, 'Dungface,' what can
the workers expect?"

- What is your immediate response to this question?
- Why do you think you responded in this way?
- Think back to the time or season when you first said yes to following Christ. What were your expectations of the Christian
  life? Who or where did they come from?
- How have your expectations matched up with reality?
- Read the passage again. When was the last time someone
  smeared your reputation or impugned your motives? When was
  the last time someone tried to silence you? Have you ever been
  called a "name" for Christ's sake?

READ

From *The Final Beast*, by Frederick Buechner[1]

That afternoon rain had soaked him until you could see the flesh through his shirt. A silent truck driver with a mouthful of popcorn had taken him part of the way, letting him off at a crook in the road by a gravel pit where he took shelter under a lean-to until a boy in chinos and a T-shirt stopped and beckoned him in; by then he no longer cringed through the downpour but sauntered out, grinning. "Christ, you been swimming the channel?" The boy's smooth jaws were working at something as he spoke. . . . "I don't go in for hitchhikers much. Sometimes they're sex fiends or something," and Nicolet, his face still dripping, replied, "I'm a minister." Then the boy had flushed, swallowing whatever it was, and for a mile there was nothing but the tick-tock of the windshield wiper until at last the boy said, "No sweat, what makes a guy decide to be a thing like that?"

"Well, there are three steps," Nicolet had said distractedly. . . . "The first step is to be a beer drinker or at least the friend of beer drinkers. It helps anyway." . . . "It was a muggy spring evening after exams," he said, "and I was tossing off a few with some of these beer-drinking friends of mine when the subject got around to religion as it usually does in such cases. . . . There was one character there who had pimples all over his chin like jam. You kept wanting to wipe it off for him." . . . Anyway, he went on, "He'd been getting sloppier and sloppier, this pimply one. Everything was four letter words. It was really quite funny for a while in a dismal kind of way. Especially when he got into one particular rut. Eats it. You know army slang? Everything was eats it. His girl friend. His roommate. The faculty. They all ate it. It. 'It . . . Eats it,'" Nicolet said. "'The great fecal indictment.' It's all he could say. I suppose I should have been able to see what was coming next, but I didn't. We'd gotten on religion, I told you. Well, he suddenly said a memorable thing, an epic thing—at least it was to me. . . . What he said was very simple. He just put together two things I'd never heard put together before. One of them was eats it. . . . And Jesus Christ . . . That was the other thing he said. According to him, Christ eats it too. . . . Christ does eat it, of course. You know why?" The boy shook his head. "Because it's all this world has ever given him to eat. And yet he keeps coming back for more."

THINK   "If they call me, the Master, 'Dungface,' what can the workers expect?"

- Buechner takes name-calling one step further. He has Jesus as the one who eats the dung of the world and keeps coming back for more. What is your reaction to this description?
- If the workers shouldn't expect more than the Master got, what does that say about at least some of the days of our lives?
- Jesus said, "It is not success you are after in such times but survival. Be survivors!" (Matthew 10:23). What are these "such times" for you? Is "survival" what you're after in these such times? Or are you after something else? If so, what?

READ

From *People of the Lie*, by M. Scott Peck[2]

I cannot be any more specific about the methodology of love than to quote these words of an old priest who spent many years in the battle: "There are dozens of ways to deal with evil and several ways to conquer it. All of them are facets of the truth that the only ultimate way to conquer evil is to let it be smothered within a willing, living human being. When it is absorbed there like blood in a sponge or a spear into one's heart, it loses its power and goes no further."

The healing of evil—scientifically or otherwise—can be accomplished only by the love of individuals. A willing sacrifice is required. The individual healer must allow his or her own soul to become the battleground. He or she must sacrificially absorb the evil.

Then what prevents the destruction of the soul? If one takes the evil itself into one's heart, like a spear, how can one's goodness still survive? Even if the evil is vanquished thereby, will not the good be also? What will have been achieved beyond some meaningless trade-off? I cannot answer this in language other than mystical. I can only say that there is a mysterious alchemy whereby the victim becomes the victor. As C. S. Lewis wrote: "When a willing victim who had committed no treachery was killed in a traitor's stead, the Table would crack and Death itself would start working backwards."

I do not know how this occurs. But I know that it does. . . . Whenever this happens there is a slight shift in the balance of power in the world.

THINK   "If they call me, the Master, 'Dungface,' what can the workers expect?"

- "The only ultimate way to conquer evil is to let it be smothered within a willing, living human being." Agree? Disagree? Unsure?

- Can you recall a time when someone influential in your life *willingly* absorbed evil, like "blood in a sponge or a spear into one's heart"? Was anything destroyed in the process? Did any goodness survive? Or is this mystical language just words on a page?
- What about you? Have you ever been willing to absorb the evil? Explain.

READ

Romans 8:31-39

So, what do you think? With God on our side like this, how can we lose? If God didn't hesitate to put everything on the line for us, embracing our condition and exposing himself to the worst by sending his own Son, is there anything else he wouldn't gladly and freely do for us? And who would dare tangle with God by messing with one of God's chosen? Who would dare even to point a finger? The One who died for us—who was raised to life for us!—is in the presence of God at this very moment sticking up for us. Do you think anyone is going to be able to drive a wedge between us and Christ's love for us? There is no way! Not trouble, not hard times, not hatred, not hunger, not homelessness, not bullying threats, not backstabbing, not even the worst sins listed in Scripture:

> They kill us in cold blood because they hate you.
> We're sitting ducks; they pick us off one by one.

None of this fazes us because Jesus loves us. I'm absolutely convinced that nothing—nothing living or dead, angelic or demonic, today or tomorrow, high or low, thinkable or unthinkable— absolutely *nothing* can get between us and God's love because of the way that Jesus our Master has embraced us.

THINK "If they call me, the Master, 'Dungface,' what can the workers expect?"

- Do you really believe God is on your side—at this very moment? Why or why not? What difference has that made in your life over, say, the last month?
- "Not trouble, not hard times, not hatred, not hunger, not homelessness, not bullying threats, not backstabbing . . . None of this fazes us because Jesus loves us." What if just one of the

things on this list happened to you this week? Would it faze you? And if it did, how do you reconcile that with the belief that God is on your side?

- Does God promise we won't be fazed by difficult things, or does he promise we'll have a way to get through them? Or something else? What is the difference between these?
- What hope or truth gives you strength to get through the times when others call you "dungface" or otherwise defame or talk badly about you?

PRAY

Look back at the "Think" sections. Ruminate on your responses. Let them distill into a prayer, and then write that prayer below.

O Love that will not let me go . . .

The issue of prayer is not prayer; the issue of prayer is God.

ABRAHAM HESCHEL

LIVE   "If they call me, the Master, 'Dungface,' what can the
                  workers expect?"

The challenge now is to take this question further along—to live out
this question. Think of one thing, *just one*, that you can personally do
to wrestle with the question, inhabit the character of it, and live it in
everyday life. In the following space, jot down your thoughts on this
"one thing." Read the Scripture and quotes that follow for additional
inspiration. During the coming week, pray about this "one thing," talk
with a close friend about it, and learn to live the question.

One thing . . .

"Not only that—count yourselves blessed every time people
put you down or throw you out or speak lies about you to
discredit me. What it means is that the truth is too close for
comfort and they are uncomfortable. You can be glad when
that happens—give a cheer, even!—for though they don't
like it, *I* do! And all heaven applauds. And know that you are
in good company. My prophets and witnesses have always
gotten into this kind of trouble."

                                                  Matthew 5:11-12

Jonathan Seagull spent the rest of his days alone, but he flew
way out beyond the Far Cliffs. His sorrow was not solitude, it
was the way the other gulls refused to believe the glory of flight
that awaited them; they refused to open their eyes and see.

                          Richard Bach, *Jonathan Livingston Seagull*

Live the questions now. Perhaps you will then gradually, without
noticing it, live along some distant day into the answer.

RAINER MARIA RILKE, *LETTERS TO A YOUNG POET*

LESSON 6

"Are you tired? Worn out? Burned out on religion?"
(Matthew 11:28)

Before You Begin

Take some time to reflect and prepare your heart and mind for this study. Read the following Scripture passage. Soak up God's Word. There's no hurry. Then, when you're ready, turn the page and begin.

ROMANS 8:23-28

These sterile and barren bodies of ours are yearning for full deliverance. That is why waiting does not diminish us, any more than waiting diminishes a pregnant mother. We are enlarged in the waiting. We, of course, don't see what is enlarging us. But the longer we wait, the larger we become, and the more joyful our expectancy.

Meanwhile, the moment we get tired in the waiting, God's Spirit is right alongside helping us along. If we don't know how or what to pray, it doesn't matter. He does our praying in and for us, making prayer out of our wordless sighs, our aching groans. He knows us far better than we know ourselves, knows our pregnant condition, and keeps us present before God. That's why we can be so sure that every detail in our lives of love for God is worked into something good.

READ

Matthew 11:20-30

Next Jesus let fly on the cities where he had worked the hardest but whose people had responded the least, shrugging their shoulders and going their own way.

"Doom to you, Korazin! Doom, Bethsaida! If Tyre and Sidon had seen half of the powerful miracles you have seen, they would have been on their knees in a minute. At Judgment Day they'll get off easy compared to you. And Capernaum! With all your peacock strutting, you are going to end up in the abyss. If the people of Sodom had had your chances, the city would still be around. At Judgment Day they'll get off easy compared to you."

Abruptly Jesus broke into prayer: "Thank you, Father, Lord of heaven and earth. You've concealed your ways from sophisticates and know-it-alls, but spelled them out clearly to ordinary people. Yes, Father, that's the way you like to work."

Jesus resumed talking to the people, but now tenderly. "The Father has given me all these things to do and say. This is a unique Father-Son operation, coming out of Father and Son intimacies and knowledge. No one knows the Son the way the Father does, nor the Father the way the Son does. But I'm not keeping it to myself; I'm ready to go over it line by line with anyone willing to listen.

"**Are you tired? Worn out? Burned out on religion?** Come to me. Get away with me and you'll recover your life. I'll show you how to take a real rest. Walk with me and work with me—watch how I do it. Learn the unforced rhythms of grace. I won't lay anything heavy or ill-fitting on you. Keep company with me and you'll learn to live freely and lightly."

THINK   "Are you tired? Worn out? Burned out on religion?"

- What is your immediate response to these questions?
- Why do you think you responded in this way?

- Have you, like Jesus, worked your hardest on some people who have been the least responsive? Would you like to "let fly" on them? Have you ever?
- Answer Jesus' questions. Honestly now, are you tired? Worn out? Burned out on religion? If so, has this come about recently in your life (some event) or has this been brewing for some time (process)?
- Jesus finishes off the passage with an invitation: "Come to me. Get away with me. . . . Learn the unforced rhythms of grace." What does it sound like he's inviting you to do? How do you do this?

READ

From *A Prayer for Owen Meany*, by John Irving[1]

Owen disliked the Episcopalians, too, but he disliked them far less than he had disliked the Catholics; in his opinion, both of them believed *less* than he believed—but the Catholics had interfered with Owen's beliefs and practices *more*. He was my best friend, and with our best friends we overlook many differences; but it wasn't until we found ourselves attending the same Sunday school, and the same church, that I was forced to accept that my best friend's religious faith was more certain (if not always more dogmatic) than anything I heard in either the Congregational or the Episcopal Church.

I don't remember Sunday school in the Congregational Church at all—although my mother claimed that this was always an occasion whereat I ate a lot, both in Sunday school and at various parish-house functions. I vaguely remember the cider and the cookies; but I remember emphatically—with a crisp, winter-day brightness—the white clapboard church, the black steeple clock, and the services that were always held on the second floor of an informal, well-lit, meetinghouse atmosphere. You could look out the tall windows at the branches of the towering trees. By comparison, the Episcopal services were conducted in a gloomy, basement atmosphere. It was a stone church, and there was a ground-floor or even underground mustiness to the place, which was overcrowded with darkwood bric-a-brac, somber with dull gold organ pipes, garish with confused configurations of stained glass—through which not a single branch of a tree was visible.

When I complained about church, I complained about the usual things a kid complains about: the claustrophobia, the boredom. But Owen complained *religiously*. "A PERSON'S FAITH GOES AT ITS OWN PACE," Owen Meany said. "THE TROUBLE WITH CHURCH IS THE SERVICE. A SERVICE IS CONDUCTED FOR A MASS AUDIENCE. JUST WHEN I START TO LIKE THE

HYMN, EVERYONE PLOPS DOWN TO PRAY. JUST WHEN I START TO HEAR THE PRAYER, EVERYONE POPS UP TO SING. AND WHAT DOES THE STUPID SERMON HAVE TO DO WITH GOD? WHO KNOWS WHAT GOD THINKS OF CURRENT EVENTS? WHO CARES?"

THINK   "Are you tired? Worn out? Burned out on religion?"

- Owen Meany gave us his opinion about church. What do *you* not like about church/religion? Here's your chance to complain "religiously"; go for it. Line up your complaints, and as the old hymn instructed, "Name them one by one."
- Now reverse the question. What do you *like* about church/religion?
- What do these lists tell you about your current feelings toward church?
- How does where you stand on these things today compare to earlier in your life? If there is a difference, what brought about that change?

READ

From *Holy the Firm*, by Annie Dillard[2]

There is one church here, so I go to it. On Sunday mornings
I quit the house and wander down the hill to the white frame
church in the firs. On a big Sunday there might be twenty of us
there; often I am the only person under sixty, and feel as though
I'm on an archaeological tour of Soviet Russia. The members are
of mixed denominations; the minister is a Congregationalist, and
wears a white shirt. The man knows God. . . .

The churchwomen all bring flowers for the altar; they haul
in arrangements as big as hedges, of wayside herbs in season,
and flowers from their gardens, huge bunches of foliage and
blossoms as tall as I am, in vases the size of tubs, and the altar
still looks empty, irredeemably linoleum, and beige. We had a
wretched singer once, a guest from a Canadian congregation,
a hulking blond girl with chopped hair and big shoulders, who
wore tinted spectacles and a long lacy dress, and sang, grinning, to faltering accompaniment, an entirely secular song about
mountains. Nothing could have been more apparent than that
God loved this girl; nothing could more surely convince me of
God's unending mercy than the continued existence on earth of
the church.

The higher Christian churches—where, if anywhere, I
belong—come at God with an unwarranted air of professional-
ism, with authority and pomp, as though they knew what they
were doing, as though people in themselves were an appropriate
set of creatures to have dealings with God. I often think of the
set pieces of liturgy as certain words which people have success-
fully addressed to God without their getting killed. In the high
churches they saunter through the liturgy like Mohawks along a
strand of scaffolding who have long since forgotten their danger.
If God were to blast such a service to bits, the congregation would
be, I believe, genuinely shocked. But in the low churches you
expect it at any minute. This is the beginning of wisdom.

THINK   "Are you tired? Worn out? Burned out on religion?"

- What's your initial response to this? What do you agree with here, and what causes you some alarm?
- What would it look like for you to bring the same whole-heartedness to your understanding of church that Annie Dillard does?
- What is "the beginning of wisdom" for you relating to church and religion?
- If you are indeed "worn out" on religion, what responsibility do you have to change that? What part of that responsibility belongs to the church?

READ

1 Samuel 17:34-36,38-40

David said, "I've been a shepherd, tending sheep for my father. Whenever a lion or bear came and took a lamb from the flock, I'd go after it, knock it down, and rescue the lamb. If it turned on me, I'd grab it by the throat, wring its neck, and kill it. Lion or bear, it made no difference—I killed it." . . .

Then Saul outfitted David as a soldier in armor. He put his bronze helmet on his head and belted his sword on him over the armor. David tried to walk but he could hardly budge.

David told Saul, "I can't even move with all this stuff on me. I'm not used to this." And he took it all off.

Then David took his shepherd's staff, selected five smooth stones from the brook, and put them in the pocket of his shepherd's pack, and with his sling in his hand approached Goliath.

THINK   *"Are you tired? Worn out? Burned out on religion?"*

- In what ways, if any, have you been trying to wear someone else's (maybe a parent's, friend's, popular author's) armor in your journey of faith?
- Has it awakened you, or left you tired? Has it turned you on, or worn you out? Has it sparked passion in you, or burned you out?
- What would it take to get you to take off the armor and recover *your* life of faith? Remember, God wants you to "live freely and lightly" (Matthew 11:30).

READ

From *Lake Wobegon Days*, by Garrison Keillor[3]

The Cox Brethren of St. Cloud held to the same doctrines as we did but they were not so exclusive, more trusting of the world—for example, several families owned television sets. They kept them in their living rooms, out in the open, and on Sunday, after meeting and before dinner, the dad might say, "Well, I wonder what's on," knowing perfectly well what was on, and turn it on—a Green Bay Packers game—and watch it. On Sunday.

I ate a few Sunday dinners at their houses, and the first time I saw a television set in a Brethren house, I was dumbfounded. None of the Wobegonian Brethren had one; we were told that watching television was the same as going to the movies—no, in other words. I wondered why the St. Cloud people were unaware of the danger. You start getting entangled in the things of the world, and one thing leads to another. First it's television, then it's worldly books, and the next thing you know, God's people are sitting around drinking whiskey sours in dim smoky bars with waitresses in skimpy black outfits. . . .

That was not my view but my parents'. . . . Small things led to bigger ones. One road leads up, the other down. A man cannot serve two masters. Dancing was out, even the Virginia reel: it led to carnal desires. Card-playing was out, which led to gambling, though we did have Rook and Flinch—why those and not pinochle? "Because. They're different." No novels, which tended to glamorize iniquity. "How do you know if you don't read them?" I asked, but they knew. "You only have to touch a stove once to know it's hot," Mother said. . . . Rock 'n' roll, jazz, swing, dance music, nightclub singing: all worldly. "How about Beethoven?" I asked, having heard something of his in school. "That depends," she said. "Was he a Christian?" . . .

On the long Sunday-night drive home, leaning forward from the back seat, I pressed them on inconsistencies like a little prosecutor: if dancing leads to carnal desire, how about holding hands? Is it wrong to put your arm around a girl? People gamble on football: is football wrong? Can you say "darn"? What if your teacher told you to read a novel? Or a short story? What if you were hitch-hiking in a blizzard and were picked up by a guy who was listening to rock 'n' roll on the radio, should you get out of the car even though you would freeze to death? "I guess the smart thing would be to dress warmly in the first place," offered Dad.

THINK   *"Are you tired? Worn out? Burned out on religion?"*

- A good gauge of the lightness in your relationship with Jesus is your ability to laugh, especially at religious things. What about this excerpt is funny to you? Why?
- What are the practices that tend to burn people out on religion? How does having a sense of humor help reduce the burnout?
- If you were to write a similar story about your church experience, highlighting those things that cause you to be worn out, what would you say?

PRAY

Look back at the "Think" sections. Ruminate on your responses.
Let them distill into a prayer, and then write that prayer below.

Jesus, I want . . .

The issue of prayer is not prayer; the issue of prayer is God.
ABRAHAM HESCHEL

LIVE

"Are you tired? Worn out? Burned out on religion?"

The challenge now is to take this question further along—to live out this question. Think of one thing, *just one*, that you can personally do to wrestle with the question, inhabit the character of it, and live it in everyday life. In the following space, jot down your thoughts on this "one thing." Read the Scripture and quotes that follow for additional inspiration. During the coming week, pray about this "one thing," talk with a close friend about it, and learn to live the question.

One thing . . .

Walking along the beach of Lake Galilee, Jesus saw two brothers: Simon (later called Peter) and Andrew. They were fishing, throwing their nets into the lake. It was their regular work. Jesus said to them, "Come with me. . . ." They didn't ask questions, but simply dropped their nets and followed.
                                                          Matthew 4:18-20

"You know that the antidote to exhaustion is not necessarily rest?"

"The antidote to exhaustion is not necessarily rest," I repeated woodenly, as if I might exhaust myself completely before I reached the end of the sentence. "What is it, then?"

"The antidote to exhaustion is wholeheartedness."
                                         David White, *Crossing the Unknown Sea*

Live the questions now. Perhaps you will then gradually, without noticing it, live along some distant day into the answer.
RAINER MARIA RILKE, *LETTERS TO A YOUNG POET*

"What kind of deal is it to get everything you want but lose yourself? What could you ever trade your soul for?"
(Matthew 16:26)

Before You Begin

Take some time to reflect and prepare your heart and mind for this study. Read the following Scripture passage. Soak up God's Word. There's no hurry. Then, when you're ready, turn the page and begin.

HEBREWS 13:20-21

May God, who puts all things together,
    makes all things whole,
Who made a lasting mark through the sacrifice of Jesus,
    the sacrifice of blood that sealed the eternal covenant,
Who led Jesus, our Great Shepherd,
    up and alive from the dead,
Now put you together, provide you
    with everything you need to please him,
Make us into what gives him most pleasure,
    by means of the sacrifice of Jesus, the Messiah.
All glory to Jesus forever and always!
    Oh, yes, yes, yes.

READ

Matthew 16:21-28

Then Jesus made it clear to his disciples that it was now necessary for him to go to Jerusalem, submit to an ordeal of suffering at the hands of the religious leaders, be killed, and then on the third day be raised up alive. Peter took him in hand, protesting, "Impossible, Master! That can never be!"

But Jesus didn't swerve. "Peter, get out of my way. Satan, get lost. You have no idea how God works."

Then Jesus went to work on his disciples. "Anyone who intends to come with me has to let me lead. You're not in the driver's seat; *I* am. Don't run from suffering; embrace it. Follow me and I'll show you how. Self-help is no help at all. Self-sacrifice is the way, my way, to finding yourself, your true self. **What kind of deal is it to get everything you want but lose yourself? What could you ever trade your soul for?**

"Don't be in such a hurry to go into business for yourself. Before you know it the Son of Man will arrive with all the splendor of his Father, accompanied by an army of angels. You'll get everything you have coming to you, a personal gift. This isn't pie in the sky by and by. Some of you standing here are going to see it take place, see the Son of Man in kingdom glory."

THINK "What kind of deal is it to get everything you want but lose yourself? What could you ever trade your soul for?"

- What is your immediate response to these questions?
- Why do you think you responded in this way?
- There is an entire culture (maybe of which you are a part) that pursues the "true self." What does that phrase mean to you?
- For now, go ahead and give the Sunday school answer. What does Jesus say is the way to finding that "true self"?
- Like most Sunday school answers, this one has been

manipulated to mean just about anything anyone wants it to mean. What does it mean to you, and how has it played out in your life?

READ

From *The Gift of the Magi*, by O. Henry[1]

Now, there were two possessions of the James Dillingham Youngs in which they both took a mighty pride. One was Jim's gold watch that had been his father's and his grandfather's. The other was Della's hair. Had the Queen of Sheba lived in the flat across the airshaft, Della would have let her hair hang out the window some day to dry just to depreciate Her majesty's jewels and gifts. Had King Solomon been the janitor, with all his treasures piled up in the basement, Jim would have pulled out his watch every time he passed, just to see him pluck at his beard from envy. . . .

Where she stopped the sign read: "Mne. Sofronie. Hair Goods of All Kinds." One flight up Della ran, and collected herself, panting. Madame, large, too white, chilly, hardly looked the "Sofronie."

"Will you buy my hair?" asked Della.

"I buy hair," said Madame. "Take yer hat off and let's have a sight at the looks of it."

Down rippled the brown cascade.

"Twenty dollars," said Madame, lifting the mass with a practised hand.

"Give it to me quick," said Della. . . .

Jim drew a package from his overcoat pocket and threw it upon the table.

"Don't make any mistake, Dell," he said, "about me. I don't think there's anything in the way of a haircut or a shave or a shampoo that could make me like my girl any less. But if you'll unwrap that package you may see why you had me going a while at first."

White fingers and nimble tore at the string and paper. And then an ecstatic scream of joy; and then, alas! a quick feminine change to hysterical tears and wails, necessitating the immediate employment of all the comforting powers of the lord of the flat. For there lay The Combs—the set of combs, side and back, that

Della had worshipped for long in a Broadway window. Beautiful combs, pure tortoise shell, with jeweled rims—just the shade to wear in the beautiful vanished hair. They were expensive combs, she knew, and her heart had simply craved and yearned over them without the least hope of possession. And now, they were hers, but the tresses that should have adorned the coveted adornments were gone.

But she hugged them to her bosom, and at length she was able to look up with dim eyes and a smile and say: "My hair grows so fast, Jim!"

And then Della leaped up like a little singed cat and cried, "Oh, oh!"

Jim had not yet seen his beautiful present. She held it out to him eagerly upon her open palm. The dull precious metal seemed to flash with a reflection of her bright and ardent spirit.

"Isn't it a dandy, Jim? I hunted all over town to find it. You'll have to look at the time a hundred times a day now. Give me your watch. I want to see how it looks on it."

Instead of obeying, Jim tumbled down on the couch and put his hands under the back of his head and smiled.

"Dell," said he, "let's put our Christmas presents away and keep 'em a while. They're too nice to use just at present. I sold the watch to get the money to buy your combs. And now suppose you put the chops on."

The magi, as you know, were wise men—wonderfully wise men—who brought gifts to the Babe in the manger. . . . And here I have lamely related to you the uneventful chronicle of two foolish children in a flat who most unwisely sacrificed for each other the greatest treasures of their house.

THINK "What kind of deal is it to get everything you want but lose yourself? What could you ever trade your soul for?"

• Whether a new story or one you heard as a child, how does this story of "two foolish children" make you feel?

- What is a possession in which you take "a mighty pride"?
- Think about the fact that Jim was known for his watch and Della known for her hair; they were pieces of identity. How does your "possession" identify you?

READ

Genesis 22:1-12,15-17

After all this, God tested Abraham. God said, "Abraham!"

"Yes?" answered Abraham. "I'm listening."

He said, "Take your dear son Isaac whom you love and go to the land of Moriah. Sacrifice him there as a burnt offering on one of the mountains that I'll point out to you."

Abraham got up early in the morning and saddled his donkey. He took two of his young servants and his son Isaac. He had split wood for the burnt offering. He set out for the place God had directed him. On the third day he looked up and saw the place in the distance. Abraham told his two young servants, "Stay here with the donkey. The boy and I are going over there to worship; then we'll come back to you."

Abraham took the wood for the burnt offering and gave it to Isaac his son to carry. He carried the flint and the knife. The two of them went off together.

Isaac said to Abraham his father, "Father?"

"Yes, my son."

"We have flint and wood, but where's the sheep for the burnt offering?"

Abraham said, "Son, God will see to it that there's a sheep for the burnt offering." And they kept on walking together.

They arrived at the place to which God had directed him. Abraham built an altar. He laid out the wood. Then he tied up Isaac and laid him on the wood. Abraham reached out and took the knife to kill his son.

Just then an angel of God called to him out of Heaven, "Abraham! Abraham!"

"Yes, I'm listening."

"Don't lay a hand on that boy! Don't touch him! Now I know how fearlessly you fear God; you didn't hesitate to place your son, your dear son, on the altar for me." . . .

The angel of God spoke from Heaven a second time to

Abraham: "I swear—GOD's sure word!—because you have gone through with this, and have not refused to give me your son, your dear, dear son, I'll bless you—oh, how I'll bless you!"

THINK   "What kind of deal is it to get everything you want but lose yourself? What could you ever trade your soul for?"

- This has been called a "terror text" by some. If you lay aside the usual religious coverings, how does this passage make you feel?
- How does this passage make you feel about God?
- Has God ever asked you to sacrifice something or someone "dear"? Did God provide a "sheep," or did you have to go through with it?
- The theme of sacrifice is huge in the Bible. How does that compare with the theme of sacrifice in your own life? What practical impact would a better understanding of the sacrifice Jesus asks for have on your everyday life?

READ

Hebrews 10:11-16

Every priest goes to work at the altar each day, offers the same old sacrifices year in, year out, and never makes a dent in the sin problem. As a priest, Christ made a single sacrifice for sins, and that was it! Then he sat down right beside God and waited for his enemies to cave in. It was a perfect sacrifice by a perfect person to perfect some very imperfect people. By that single offering, he did everything that needed to be done for everyone who takes part in the purifying process. The Holy Spirit confirms this:

> This new plan I'm making with Israel
>> isn't going to be written on paper,
>> isn't going to be chiseled in stone;
> This time "I'm writing out the plan *in* them,
>> carving it on the lining of their hearts."

THINK   "What kind of deal is it to get everything you want but lose yourself? What could you ever trade your soul for?"

- Does the act of giving up "everything you want" happen once, or is it an ongoing sacrifice?
- When you consider the sacrifice Jesus asks of you in light of the sacrifice he made, what is your immediate reaction to that comparison?
- If Jesus "did everything that needed to be done for everyone" in his sacrifice, why does he still ask us to live sacrificially?
- How did Jesus' sacrifice help to define your identity? How do your daily choices not to "trade your soul" assist in that definition?

PRAY

Look back at the "Think" sections. Ruminate on your responses. Let them distill into a prayer, and then write that prayer below.

Guide me, o thou Great Jehovah . . .

The issue of prayer is not prayer; the issue of prayer is God.

ABRAHAM HESCHEL

LIVE   "What kind of deal is it to get everything you want but lose yourself? What could you ever trade your soul for?"

The challenge now is to take this question further along—to live out this question. Think of one thing, *just one*, that you can personally do to wrestle with the question, inhabit the character of it, and live it in everyday life. In the following space, jot down your thoughts on this "one thing." Read the Scripture and quotes that follow for additional inspiration. During the coming week, pray about this "one thing," talk with a close friend about it, and learn to live the question.

One thing . . .

If Abraham had doubted as he stood there on Mount Moriah, if irresolute he had looked around, if he had happened to spot the ram before drawing the knife, if God had allowed him to sacrifice it instead of Isaac—then he would have gone home, everything would have been the same, he would have Sarah, he would have kept Isaac, and yet how changed! For his return would have been a flight, his deliverance an accident, his reward disgrace, his future perhaps perdition. Then he would have witnessed neither to his faith nor to God's grace but would have witnessed to how appalling it is to go to Mount Moriah.

Soren Kierkegaard, *Fear and Trembling*

At best we do not sacrifice ourselves for others; we help others and we sharpen and define ourselves as we make choices. We sacrifice some things we could be for other things, and in this way create, carve out a self, an identity. . . . Making a choice . . . helps me define what is most important to me . . . and hence to know more about who I am.

Carol Pearson, *The Hero Within*

Live the questions now. Perhaps you will then gradually, without noticing it, live along some distant day into the answer.
RAINER MARIA RILKE, *LETTERS TO A YOUNG POET*

"Do you have any idea how difficult it is for the rich to enter God's kingdom?" (Matthew 19:23)

Before You Begin

Take some time to reflect and prepare your heart and mind for this study. Read the following Scripture passage. Soak up God's Word. There's no hurry. Then, when you're ready, turn the page and begin.

Psalms 49:16-19

So don't be impressed with those who get rich
    and pile up fame and fortune.
They can't take it with them;
    fame and fortune all get left behind.
Just when they think they've arrived
    and folks praise them because they've made good,
They enter the family burial plot
    where they'll never see sunshine again.

READ

Matthew 19:16-24

Another day, a man stopped Jesus and asked, "Teacher, what good thing must I do to get eternal life?"

Jesus said, "Why do you question me about what's good? *God* is the One who is good. If you want to enter the life of God, just do what he tells you."

The man asked, "What in particular?"

Jesus said, "Don't murder, don't commit adultery, don't steal, don't lie, honor your father and mother, and love your neighbor as you do yourself."

The young man said, "I've done all that. What's left?"

"If you want to give it all you've got," Jesus replied, "go sell your possessions; give everything to the poor. All your wealth will then be in heaven. Then come follow me."

That was the last thing the young man expected to hear. And so, crestfallen, he walked away. He was holding on tight to a lot of things, and he couldn't bear to let go.

As he watched him go, Jesus told his disciples, "**Do you have any idea how difficult it is for the rich to enter God's kingdom?** Let me tell you, it's easier to gallop a camel through a needle's eye than for the rich to enter God's kingdom."

THINK   *"Do you have any idea how difficult it is for the rich to enter God's kingdom?"*

- What is your immediate response to this question?
- Why do you think you responded in this way?
- What is your impression of the man who stops and asks Jesus a question?
- "I've done all that. What's left?" Do you know anyone who resembles this young man?
- If "good" things do not get us "eternal life," then what is Jesus saying to this young man?
- What do you feel for the young man by the end of the passage?

THINK (continued)

READ

From *Walden*, by Henry David Thoreau[1]

The very simplicity and nakedness of man's life in the primitive ages imply this advantage, at least, that they left him still but a sojourner in nature. When he was refreshed with food and sleep he contemplated his journey again. He dwelt, as it were, in a tent in this world, and was either threading the valleys, or crossing the plains, or climbing the mountaintops. But lo! Men have become tools of their tools. The man who independently plucked the fruits when he was hungry is become a farmer, and he who stood under a tree for shelter, a housekeeper. We now no longer camp as for a night, but have settled down on earth and forgotten heaven. We have adopted Christianity merely as an improved method of agriculture. We have built for this world a family mansion, and for the next a family tomb.

From *The Hidden Wound*, by Wendell Berry[2]

As Thoreau so well knew, and so painstakingly tried to show us, what a man most needs is not a knowledge of how to get more, but a knowledge of the most he can do without, and of how to get along without it. The essential cultural discrimination is not between having and not having or haves and have-nots, but between the superfluous and the indispensable. Wisdom, it seems to me, is always poised upon the knowledge of minimums; it might be thought to be the art of minimums. Granting the frailty, and no doubt the impermanence, of modern technology as a human contrivance, the man who can keep a fire in a stove or on a hearth is not only more durable, but wiser, closer to the meaning of fire, than the man who can only work a thermostat.

THINK   "Do you have any idea how difficult it is for the rich to enter God's kingdom?"

- Thoreau talks of settling down on earth and forgetting heaven. When was the last time you really thought about heaven?
- Would you consider yourself fairly settled in life right now? Are you doing what you want to do? Living where you want to live? Driving what you want to drive?
- Wendell Berry speaks of the knowledge or "art of minimums." What is your reaction to his words?
- If someone asked you for a list right now entitled "The Minimums for My Life," what would be on your list?

READ

From *In the Name of Jesus*, by Henri Nouwen[3]

> The Christian leader of the future needs to be radically poor, journeying with nothing except a staff—"no bread, no haversack, no money, no spare tunic" (Mark 6:8). What is good about being poor? Nothing, except that it offers us the possibility of giving leadership by allowing ourselves to be led. We will become dependent on the positive or negative responses of those to whom we go and thus be truly led to where the Spirit of Jesus wants to lead us. Wealth and riches prevent us from truly discerning the way of Jesus. Paul writes to Timothy: "People who long to be rich are a prey to trial; they get trapped into all sorts of foolish and harmful ambitions which plunge people into ruin and destruction" (1 Timothy 6:9). If there is any hope for the Church in the future, it will be hope for a poor Church."

THINK   "Do you have any idea how difficult it is for the rich to enter God's kingdom?"

- "Wealth and riches prevent us from truly discerning the way of Jesus." What if this statement didn't apply to just Christian leaders? What if it applied to Christians, such as you?
- In what ways do you see yourself "trapped into all sorts of foolish and harmful ambitions" because of your desire for riches?
- What difference would it make in the way you are living right now if you followed Nouwen's advice? (And remember, there are those who *have* wealth and riches and there are those who *pursue* wealth and riches.)

READ

From *Celebration of Discipline*, by Richard Foster[4]

He exhorted the rich young ruler not just to have an inner attitude of detachment from his possessions, but literally to get rid of his possessions if he wanted the kingdom of God (Matt. 19:16-22). He says, "Take heed, and beware of all covetousness; for a man's life does not consist in the abundance of his possessions" (Luke 12:15). He counseled people who came seeking God, "Sell your possessions, and give alms; provide yourselves with purses that do not grow old, with a treasure in the heavens that does not fail" (Luke 12:33). He told the parable of the rich farmer whose life centered on hoarding—we would call him prudent; Jesus called him a fool (Luke 12:16-21). He states that if we really want the kingdom of God we must, like a merchant in search of fine pearls, be willing to sell everything we have to get it (Matt. 13:45,46). He calls all who would follow him to a joyful life of carefree unconcern for possessions: "Give to everyone who begs from you; and of him who takes away your goods do not ask them again" (Luke 6:30). Jesus speaks to the questions of economics more than any other single social issue. If, in a comparatively simple society, our Lord lays such strong emphasis upon the spiritual dangers of wealth, how much more should we who live in a highly affluent culture take seriously the economic question.

THINK "Do you have any idea how difficult it is for the rich to enter God's kingdom?"

- Do Foster's words sound radical to you?
- What do you agree with? Disagree with?
- How often do you take seriously the "questions of economics"? How often does your family? Your church?
- If you answered, "Rarely," to any of the questions above, ask yourself why.

THINK (continued)

READ

From "I'd Rather Have Jesus," by Rhea F. Miller[5]

> I'd rather have Jesus than silver or gold;
> I'd rather be His than have riches untold;
> I'd rather have Jesus than houses or lands.
> I'd rather be led by His nail-pierced hand
> Than to be the king of a vast domain
> Or be held in sin's dread sway.
> I'd rather have Jesus than anything
> This world affords today.
>
> I'd rather have Jesus than men's applause;
> I'd rather be faithful to His dear cause;
> I'd rather have Jesus than worldwide fame.
> I'd rather be true to His holy name
> Than to be the king of a vast domain
> Or be held in sin's dread sway.
> I'd rather have Jesus than anything
> This world affords today.
>
> He's fairer than lilies of rarest bloom;
> He's sweeter than honey from out the comb;
> He's all that my hungering spirit needs.
> I'd rather have Jesus and let Him lead
> Than to be the king of a vast domain
> Or be held in sin's dread sway.
> I'd rather have Jesus than anything
> This world affords today.

THINK "Do you have any idea how difficult it is for the rich to enter God's kingdom?"

- Would you *really* rather have Jesus than the things mentioned in the words of this hymn?

- The third verse talks about a "hungering spirit." Describe your spirit right now. Hungering? Content? Dulled?
- What would it take for you to truly desire Jesus above all the "stuff" that defines your life today?

PRAY

Look back at the "Think" sections. Ruminate on your responses. Let them distill into a prayer, and then write that prayer below.

Son of God, Son of Man . . .

The issue of prayer is not prayer; the issue of prayer is God.

ABRAHAM HESCHEL

LIVE   "Do you have any idea how difficult it is for the rich to enter God's kingdom?"

The challenge now is to take this question further along—to live out this question. Think of one thing, *just one*, that you can personally do to wrestle with the question, inhabit the character of it, and live it in everyday life. In the following space, jot down your thoughts on this "one thing." Read the Scripture and quotes that follow for additional inspiration. During the coming week, pray about this "one thing," talk with a close friend about it, and learn to live the question.

One thing...

Prosperity is as short-lived as a wildflower, so don't ever count on it. You know that as soon as the sun rises, pouring down its scorching heat, the flower withers. Its petals wilt and, before you know it, that beautiful face is a barren stem. Well, that's a picture of the "prosperous life." At the very moment everyone is looking on in admiration, it fades away to nothing.

James 1:10-11

This clumsy living that moves lumbering
as if in ropes through what is not done,
reminds us of the awkward way the swan walks.

And to die, which is the letting go
of the ground we stand on and cling to every day,
is like the swan, when he nervously lets himself down
into the water, which receives him gaily
and which flows joyfully under

and after him, wave after wave,
while the swan, unmoving and marvelously calm,
is pleased to be carried, each moment more fully grown,
more like a king, further and further on.
Rainer Maria Rilke, "The Swan," translated by Robert Bly

Live the questions now. Perhaps you will then gradually, without
noting it, live along some distant day into the answer.
RAINER MARIA RILKE, *LETTERS TO A YOUNG POET*

"If someone has a hundred sheep and one of them wanders off, doesn't he leave the ninety-nine and go after the one?"
(Matthew 18:12)

Before You Begin

Take some time to reflect and prepare your heart and mind for this study. Read the following Scripture passage. Soak up God's Word. There's no hurry. Then, when you're ready, turn the page and begin.

Jeremiah 31:10

"Hear this, nations! God's Message!
     Broadcast this all over the world!
Tell them, 'The One who scattered Israel
     will gather them together again.
From now on he'll keep a careful eye on them,
     like a shepherd with his flock.'"

READ

Matthew 18:1-14

At about the same time, the disciples came to Jesus asking, "Who gets the highest rank in God's kingdom?"

For an answer Jesus called over a child, whom he stood in the middle of the room, and said, "I'm telling you, once and for all, that unless you return to square one and start over like children, you're not even going to get a look at the kingdom, let alone get in. Whoever becomes simple and elemental again, like this child, will rank high in God's kingdom. What's more, when you receive the childlike on my account, it's the same as receiving me.

"But if you give them a hard time, bullying or taking advantage of their simple trust, you'll soon wish you hadn't. You'd be better off dropped in the middle of the lake with a millstone around your neck. Doom to the world for giving these God-believing children a hard time! Hard times are inevitable, but you don't have to make it worse—and it's doomsday to you if you do.

"If your hand or your foot gets in the way of God, chop it off and throw it away. You're better off maimed or lame and alive than the proud owners of two hands and two feet, godless in a furnace of eternal fire. And if your eye distracts you from God, pull it out and throw it away. You're better off one-eyed and alive than exercising your twenty-twenty vision from inside the fire of hell.

"Watch that you don't treat a single one of these childlike believers arrogantly. You realize, don't you, that their personal angels are constantly in touch with my Father in heaven?

"Look at it this way. **If someone has a hundred sheep and one of them wanders off, doesn't he leave the ninety-nine and go after the one?** And if he finds it, doesn't he make far more over it than over the ninety-nine who stay put? Your Father in heaven feels the same way. He doesn't want to lose even one of these simple believers."

THINK   "If someone has a hundred sheep and one of them
             wanders off, doesn't he leave the ninety-nine and
             go after the one?"

- What is your immediate response to this question?
- Why do you think you responded in this way?
- What is your reaction to the idea that there's a "rank" in God's kingdom? Isn't everything equal in heaven?
- What does it mean to you to be "simple and elemental," "childlike," a "simple believer"?

READ

From *Leaving Home*, by Garrison Keillor[1]

Larry the Sad Boy was there, who was saved twelve times in the
Lutheran church, an all-time record. Between 1953 and 1961, he
threw himself weeping and contrite on God's throne of grace
on twelve separate occasions—and this is in a Lutheran church
that wasn't evangelical, had no altar call, no organist playing "Just
As I Am Without One Plea" while a choir hummed and a guy
with shiny hair took hold of your heartstrings and played you
like a cheap guitar—this is the Lutheran church, not a bunch
of hillbillies—these are Scandinavians, and they repent in the
same way they sin: discreetly, tastefully, at the proper time, and
bring a Jell-O salad for afterward. Larry Sorenson came forward
weeping buckets and crumpled up at the communion rail, to
the amazement of the minister, who had delivered a dry sermon
about stewardship, and who now had to put his arm around this
limp soggy individual and pray with him and see if he had a ride
home. *Twelve times.*

Even we fundamentalists got tired of him. Granted, we're
born in original sin and are worthless and vile, but twelve conver-
sions is too many. God didn't mean us to feel guilt all our lives.
There comes a point when you should dry your tears and join
the building committee and start grappling with the problems of
the church furnace and the church roof and make church coffee
and be of use, but Larry kept on repenting and repenting.

THINK   "If someone has a hundred sheep and one of them
wanders off, doesn't he leave the ninety-nine and
go after the one?"

- What do you feel for Larry the Sad Boy?
- What do you feel for the minister who "had to put his arm
  around this limp soggy individual and pray with him and see if
  he had a ride home"?

- Keillor never mentions anyone trying to find out what was going on in Larry's life from 1953 to 1961. He just talks about him as sad and always needing to repent. What implications does Jesus' question have for how you might respond to Larry?
- Has there been or is there a "Larry the Sad Boy" in your life? A repetitious, "soggy individual"? How have you or how are you responding to him or her?

READ

From *Little Lamb, Who Made Thee?* by Walter Wangerin Jr.[2]

In those days homesickness seemed to curl in me like a little creature deep in my bowels. When it stirred, I suffered a sweet abdominal pain, like having to go to the bathroom. . . .

In the spring of my second-grade year, several months before the school term ended, my whole family moved from Chicago, Illinois, to Grand Forks, North Dakota. My father had accepted a call to serve Immanuel Lutheran Church as its pastor. This church also maintained a parochial school. . . .

So, then, here we were in a completely new environment, a new neighborhood in which every face was strange, and even a new house, a huge house, a three-story house that made odd sounds in the night, keeping me awake with wondering.

So, then, I was completely unprepared for my mother's plans for me. . . .

But my mother said, "I think you ought to go to school." . . .

I sat in the back with the W's. Wangerin. A kid named Corky Zimbrick sat behind me.

I didn't talk. I didn't move. My face was already warm. My mother had driven away some time ago. I was alone. Danger zone. Homesickness had made itself felt in the regions of my chest. . . .

Corky Zimbrick whispered in my ear, "Who are you? Are you the preacher's kid?"

Oh, no, I was known! Someone actually knew me. It was like being snatched from hiding. I started puffing and puffing, sucking huge chestfuls of air. Homesickness was coming higher, almost too high to be controlled. . . . I sat violently still, biting my teeth together as hard as I could. That little creature, homesickness and horror, had crept higher. . . . I breathed deeply, deeply, blowing air out at the nose, staring directly at the bottom left-hand star on the American flag. . . .

But then the worst thing happened, and I lost it.

They sang a hymn.

Hymns kill you.

All the kids in the classroom started to sing, "Blest be the tie that binds/Our hearts in Christian love—," and homesickness clogged my throat and squirted out my eyes. I burst into tears, sobbing, sobbing. I put my head down on the desk and tried to at least cry quietly. But I was crying now. Nothing could stop it or console me. Nothing.

Miss Augustine called for recess. Kids began to rush outside.

"What's the matter with him? Isn't he coming?"

"Never mind," said Miss Augustine. "Never you mind, Corky Z."

So, then it was altogether still in the room. So I allowed some boo-hoos, some genuine shuddering sobs, all with my head down on my arms, down on the desktop.

Suddenly I heard humming beside me.

I peeped out underneath my arm and saw Miss Augustine sitting at the desk across the aisle from mine. She was huge in the little seat. . . .

"Walter Martin?" she said in a soft voice. "Walter Martin, do you mind if I sit here?"

I shook my head.

"Oh, thank you," she said. "Sometimes I like to sit here when I do my work."

She began to hum again. Soon the humming turned into a little song, with words: Jesus loves me, this I know—

But then, in the middle of a line, she stopped. "Walter Martin?" she said. "Walter Martin, do you mind if I sing?"

I shook my head.

"Thank you," she said. "Sometimes I like to sing when I work."

—for the Bible tells me so—

Then she said, "Walter Martin, do you know this song?"

I nodded. I did. I had learned it last summer.

She said, "Well, then, do you want to sing it with me?"

Forever and ever I will recall with admiration that Miss Augustine was not offended when I shook my head, meaning no. . . . But Miss Augustine, in her soft voice, said, "Oh, that's right.

Little boys can't sing when they're crying, can they?"

She said, "Well, but do you think we could shout the song together?"

So then the children of Immanuel Lutheran School who were playing on the playground for recess heard two voices roaring through the windows, one fully as loud as the other:

"JESUS LOVES ME, THIS I KNOW! FOR THE BIBLE TELLS ME SO—" And I screamed as loud as I could, blowing the creature of homesickness out of my throat, dispelling sorrows and fear and mournings together:

LITTLE ONES TO HIM BELONG!

THEY ARE WEAK,

BUT HE IS STRONG.

YES!

JESUS LOVES ME. YES—

THINK   "If someone has a hundred sheep and one of them wanders off, doesn't he leave the ninety-nine and go after the one?"

- Describe an experience you've had of being the "new" kid.
- Look deep into that experience. Was there a "Miss Augustine" in those scenes?
- Describe your reaction to how Miss Augustine left the ninety-nine and sought out the one.
- If there is a "Walter Martin" in your life right now, how might you reach out to him or her?

READ

From *One Time*, by William Stafford[3]

When evening had flowed between houses
and paused on the schoolground, I met
Hilary's blind little sister following
the gray smooth railing still warm from the sun
with her hand; and she stood by the edge
holding her face upward waiting
while the last light found her cheek
and her hair, and then on over the trees.

You could hear the great sprinkler arm
of water find and then leave the pavement,
and pigeons telling each other their dreams
or the dreams they would have. We were
deep in the well of shadow by then, and I
held out my hand, saying, "Tina, it's me—Hilary says I should tell
you it's dark,
and, oh, Tina, it is. Together now—"

And I reached, our hands touched,
and we found our way home.

THINK

"If someone has a hundred sheep and one of them
wanders off, doesn't he leave the ninety-nine and
go after the one?"

- Read Stafford's poem again. Try to really "see" what's going on.
- Describe any feelings you have for the two characters in the poem.
- What if Tina wasn't the lost sheep? What if the poet, William, was? Read it again with that perspective.
- When has someone helped you to find your way home? What was that experience like?

THINK (continued)

READ

From *The Ragamuffin Gospel*, by Brennan Manning[4]

Prayer is another area that many struggle with because they aren't aware that in the freedom of the Spirit there are as many ways of praying as there are individual believers. The cardinal rule in prayer remains the dictum of Don Chapman, "Pray as you can; don't pray as you can't."

Let us suppose you give your three-year-old daughter a coloring book and a box of crayons for her birthday. The following day, with the proud smile only a little one can muster, she presents her first pictures for inspection. She has colored the sun black, the grass purple, and the sky green. In the lower right-hand corner, she has added woozy wonders of floating slabs and hovering rings: on the left, a panoply of colorful, carefree squiggles. You marvel at her bold strokes and intuit that her psyche is railing against its own cosmic puniness in the face of a big, ugly world. Later at the office, you share with your staff your daughter's first artistic effort and you make veiled references to the early work of Van Gogh.

A little child cannot do a bad coloring; nor can a child of God do bad prayer. "A father is delighted when his little one, leaving off her toys and friends, runs to him and climbs into his arms. As he holds his little one close to him, he cares little whether the child is looking around, her attention flitting from one thing to another, or just settling down to sleep. Essentially the child is choosing to be with her father, confident of the love, the care, the security that is hers in those arms. Our prayer is much like that. We settle down in our Father's arms, in his loving hands. Our mind, our thoughts, our imagination may flit about here and there; we might even fall asleep; but essentially we are choosing for this time to remain intimately with our Father, giving ourselves to him, receiving his love and care, letting him enjoy us as he will. It is very simple prayer. It is very childlike prayer. It is prayer that opens us out to all the delights of the kingdom."[5]

THINK   "If someone has a hundred sheep and one of them wanders off, doesn't he leave the ninety-nine and go after the one?"

- What feelings does this passage evoke in you about God?
- What is an area of your Christian life that makes you feel inadequate, sad, maybe even homesick?
- How have you handled it? Are you trying harder? Have you given up? Have you resigned yourself to "that's just the way it is"?
- It's time to flip your perspective on Jesus' question. Now it's all about you. Can you see yourself as one the Father loves dearly; one whose "personal angels are constantly in touch with [the] Father"; one who the Father would leave the ninety-nine to find? (See first "Read" section in this lesson.) If you have trouble with this, what do you think is at the root of that difficulty?

PRAY

Look back at the "Think" sections. Ruminate on your responses. Let them distill into a prayer, and then write that prayer below.

Abba, Father . . .

The issue of prayer is not prayer; the issue of prayer is God.

ABRAHAM HESCHEL

LIVE   "If someone has a hundred sheep and one of them wanders off, doesn't he leave the ninety-nine and go after the one?"

The challenge now is to take this question further along—to live out this question. Think of one thing, *just one*, that you can personally do to wrestle with the question, inhabit the character of it, and live it in everyday life. In the following space, jot down your thoughts on this "one thing." Read the Scripture and quotes that follow for additional inspiration. During the coming week, pray about this "one thing," talk with a close friend about it, and learn to live the question.

One thing...

Lord, what I once had done with youthful might,
Had I been from the first true to the truth,
Grant me, now old, to do—with better sight,
And humbler heart, if not the brain of youth;
So wilt thou, in thy gentleness and ruth,
Lead back thy old soul, by the path of pain,
Round to his best—young eyes and heart and brain.
George MacDonald, "The Diary of an Old Soul"

The deeds you do today may be the only sermon some people will hear today.
Saint Francis of Assisi

Live the questions now. Perhaps you will then gradually, without noticing it, live along some distant day into the answer.
RAINER MARIA RILKE, *LETTERS TO A YOUNG POET*

"Do you have any idea how silly you look, writing a life story that's wrong from start to finish, nitpicking over commas and semicolons?" (Matthew 23:24)

Before You Begin

Take some time to reflect and prepare your heart and mind for this study. Read the following Scripture passage. Soak up God's Word. There's no hurry. Then, when you're ready, turn the page and begin.

MATTHEW 23:27-28

"You're hopeless, you religion scholars and Pharisees! Frauds! You're like manicured grave plots, grass clipped and the flowers bright, but six feet down it's all rotting bones and worm-eaten flesh. People look at you and think you're saints, but beneath the skin you're total frauds."

READ

Matthew 23:13-24

"I've had it with you! You're hopeless, you religion scholars, you Pharisees! Frauds! Your lives are roadblocks to God's kingdom. You refuse to enter, and won't let anyone else in either.

"You're hopeless, you religion scholars and Pharisees! Frauds! You go halfway around the world to make a convert, but once you get him you make him into a replica of yourselves, double-damned.

"You're hopeless! What arrogant stupidity! You say, 'If someone makes a promise with his fingers crossed, that's nothing; but if he swears with his hand on the Bible, that's serious.' What ignorance! Does the leather on the Bible carry more weight than the skin on your hands? And what about this piece of trivia: 'If you shake hands on a promise, that's nothing; but if you raise your hand that God is your witness, that's serious'? What ridiculous hairsplitting! What difference does it make whether you shake hands or raise hands? A promise is a promise. What difference does it make if you make your promise inside or outside a house of worship? A promise is a promise. God is present, watching and holding you to account regardless.

"You're hopeless, you religion scholars and Pharisees! Frauds! You keep meticulous account books, tithing on every nickel and dime you get, but on the meat of God's Law, things like fairness and compassion and commitment—the absolute basics!—you carelessly take it or leave it. Careful bookkeeping is commendable, but the basics are required. **Do you have any idea how silly you look, writing a life story that's wrong from start to finish, nitpicking over commas and semicolons?"**

THINK   *"Do you have any idea how silly you look, writing a life story that's wrong from start to finish, nitpicking over commas and semicolons?"*

- What is your immediate response to this question?
- Why do you think you responded in this way?
- Just so we're clear, whom is Jesus talking to?
- What would happen if someone walked into your church and started talking to your church leaders like that?
- "Hopeless," "arrogant," "stupid"—such language! Does this sound like the Jesus you're familiar with?
- Jesus says that things like fairness, compassion, and commitment are the absolute basics. How are you doing with the basics?

READ

From *Crossing to Safety*, by Wallace Stegner[1]

Morning light, without gleam or glare. The rented horse stands patiently in his aristocratic bones. . . . The bare wooden sawbuck of the packsaddle demeans his bony elegance and emphasizes his patience.

On the ground, spread out on a tarp, is what we intended to put on him—sleeping bags, pup tents, canvas bucket, axe, coils of rope, a half sack of oats, and two big pack hampers crammed with food, utensils, sweaters, slickers, and extra socks. Sid tightens and tests the cinch. Vicky, with the two infants in their shared buggy, and Barney and Nicky held back by the hand from tearing onto the tarp and disturbing its careful order, stands back with Charity and Sally. The babies are only recently weaned, and their mothers are nervous about leaving them. Aunt Emily circles, getting us into snapshot.

Sid grabs a hamper, I grab the other, and we heave them up and hang them over the forks of the saddle. But Charity, who has been giving Vicky last-minute instructions written out on two sheets of paper, looks up just then and cries out, "Wait. Wait! We have to check the list." With his hands on Wizard's neck, Sid says in his light, musical voice, "Larry and I checked it when we packed last night."

"Ah, but Pritchard says always doublecheck."

Incredulous, he stares. "You mean take everything out and repack it?"

"I don't know how else we can be sure."

"Then why did we pack it all last night?"

"I'm sure I don't know. You should have known we'd have to check."

He starts to answer, but says nothing. . . .

Incredibly, it has become a confrontation. You can feel the stubbornness in the air. It will show up in the snapshot that Aunt Emily is taking from the corner, bending over her box Brownie unwittingly recording tension.

THINK "Do you have any idea how silly you look, writing a life story that's wrong from start to finish, nitpicking over commas and semicolons?"

- Sid and Charity Lang have been married for years. This episode has played itself out countless times. Resisting the temptation to pass this off as male/female differences, are you more like Sid or Charity?
- If you said "Sid", think about a "Charity" in your life. How do you usually relate to this person?
- If you said "Charity," how has having to "always doublecheck" affected your relationships? Has it ever resulted in confrontation? If so, what did that look like?
- Is doublechecking akin to the nitpicking Jesus talks about? Explain your answer.

READ

From *The Reflective Life*, by Ken Gire[2]

The difference between an intellectual approach to the Scriptures and an intimate approach is dramatized in a scene from *The Dead Poets Society*, starring Robin Williams as Professor Keating. One of my favorite scenes in the movie is a classroom scene where Keating calls on one of his students.

"Mr. Perry, will you read the opening paragraph of the preface: 'Understanding Poetry by Dr. J. Evans Pritchart, Ph.D.'?"

The young Mr. Perry opens his book and dutifully reads. "To fully understand a poem we must be fluent in its meter, rhyme, and figures of speech. Then ask two questions: One. How artfully has the objective of the poem been rendered? Two. How important is that objective? Question one rates its perfection. Question two, its importance. Once these questions have been answered, seeing the poem's greatness is relatively easy. If the poem's score is plotted on a graph, with the vertical line representing its importance and the horizontal line its perfection, its greatness can easily be ascertained."

As the boy continues to read, Keating chalks a graph on the blackboard. The other students carefully copy it in their notebooks. After Mr. Perry finishes, Keating turns to the class, smiles, then says one word.

"Excrement."

Which takes every student off guard.

"We're not laying pipe," says Keating with mounting passion. "We're talking about poetry. Now I want you to rip out that page. The entire page. Rip it out."

The students' eyes widen.

"In fact," Keating says, "rip out the entire introduction. I want it gone. History. Be gone, J. Evans Pritchart." . . .

One by one they start ripping as Keating continues his impassioned plea.

"This is a battle, a war, and the casualties are our hearts and souls. . . . We don't read and write poetry because it's cute. We read and write poetry because we're members of the human race, and the human race is filled with passion. Medicine. Law. Business. Engineering. All noble pursuits and necessary to sustain life. But poetry, beauty, romance, love—these are what we stay alive for." . . .

The conflict between Jesus and the religious establishment was over similar ideals. Chiseled into the thinking of the scribes and Pharisees were the ideals: Law. Tradition. Ritual. Morality. Into that establishment came a teacher with no formal education and a loyal following of disciples. He espoused things that sounded very much like: Poetry. Beauty. Romance. Love.

THINK   "Do you have any idea how silly you look, writing a life story that's wrong from start to finish, nitpicking over commas and semicolons?"

- What is your reaction to the scene from *The Dead Poets Society*?
- What is your estimation of Professor Keating?
- Read through this and the Matthew passage once more. Do you see any similarities between Jesus and Keating? What about differences?
- What do you think Jesus is telling the Pharisees to rip out?
- What are some of the things you might need to rip out?

READ

From *Abba's Child*, by Brennan Manning[3]

The stakes are not small here. The Pharisees insist on the overriding importance of the rule of law. The basic dignity and genuine needs of human beings are irrelevant. Jesus, however, insisted that law was not an end in itself but the means to an end: Obedience was the expression of the love of God and neighbor, and therefore any form of piety that stood in the way of love stood in the way of God Himself. Such freedom challenged the Jewish system. Yet Jesus said He had not come to destroy the law but to fulfill it. What He offered was not a new law but a new attitude toward law based on being loving.

The pharisaic spirit flourishes today in those who use the authority of religion to control others, entangling them in unending spools of regulations, watching them struggle and refusing to assist. Eugene Kennedy asserted, "The Pharisees' power rises from the burden they heap on the backs of sincere Jews; their gratification comes out of the primitive manipulations of people's fears of displeasing their God."[4] The sign outside one Western church proclaiming "Homosexuals are not welcome" is as offensive and degrading as the sign in the window of a southern thrift store in the 1940s: "No dogs or niggers allowed!"

The words of Jesus, "What I want is mercy, not sacrifice" are addressed to men and women of religion across the boundaries of time. . . .

The Pharisee's forté in any age is blaming, accusing, and guilt-tripping others. His gift is noticing the speck in another's eye and failing to see the beam in his own. Blinded by his own ambition, the pharisee cannot see his shadow and thus projects it on others. This is his gift, his signature, his most predictable and reliable response.

THINK   "Do you have any idea how silly you look, writing
a life story that's wrong from start to finish,
nitpicking over commas and semicolons?"

- What is your response to Manning's words?
- Do you believe the pharisaic spirit still flourishes today? Where? What does it look like?
- The temptation is always to think that someone else is the one being pharisaical. What about you? Could anyone describe you as "blaming, accusing, and guilt-tripping others" as you write your life's story? Would you ever describe yourself that way?

READ

Matthew 23:25-34

"You're hopeless, you religion scholars and Pharisees! Frauds! You burnish the surface of your cups and bowls so they sparkle in the sun, while the insides are maggoty with your greed and gluttony. Stupid Pharisee! Scour the insides, and then the gleaming surface will mean something.

"You're hopeless, you religion scholars and Pharisees! Frauds! You're like manicured grave plots, grass clipped and the flowers bright, but six feet down it's all rotting bones and worm-eaten flesh. People look at you and think you're saints, but beneath the skin you're total frauds.

"You're hopeless, you religion scholars and Pharisees! Frauds! You build granite tombs for your prophets and marble monuments for your saints. And you say that if you had lived in the days of your ancestors, no blood would have been on your hands. You protest too much! You're cut from the same cloth as those murderers, and daily add to the death count.

"Snakes! Reptilian sneaks! Do you think you can worm your way out of this? Never have to pay the piper? It's on account of people like you that I send prophets and wise guides and scholars generation after generation—and generation after generation you treat them like dirt, greeting them with lynch mobs, hounding them with abuse."

THINK   "Do you have any idea how silly you look, writing a life story that's wrong from start to finish, nitpicking over commas and semicolons?"

- These are easily the most pointed words from Jesus' mouth. They were spoken to the religious community leaders. We need to hear them today, for they are meant for us.
- "Scour the insides, and then the gleaming surface will mean something." What does this phrase say to you today?

- In what ways have you lived out the sad truth in this statement: "People look at you and think you're saints, but beneath the skin you're total frauds"?
- Respond to Jesus' statement that pharisaical people are "cut from the same cloth as those murderers, and daily add to the death count."

PRAY

Look back at the "Think" sections. Ruminate on your responses. Let them distill into a prayer, and then write that prayer below.

Light of the world . . .

The issue of prayer is not prayer; the issue of prayer is God.

ABRAHAM HESCHEL

LIVE "Do you have any idea how silly you look, writing a life story that's wrong from start to finish, nitpicking over commas and semicolons?"

The challenge now is to take this question further along—to live out this question. Think of one thing, *just one*, that you can personally do to wrestle with the question, inhabit the character of it, and live it in everyday life. In the following space, jot down your thoughts on this "one thing." Read the Scripture and quotes that follow for additional inspiration. During the coming week, pray about this "one thing," talk with a close friend about it, and learn to live the question.

One thing . . .

"Yes, I'm on my way to visit you with Judgment. I'll present compelling evidence against sorcerers, adulterers, liars, those who exploit workers, those who take advantage of widows and orphans, those who are inhospitable to the homeless—anyone and everyone who doesn't honor me." A Message from God-of-the-Angel-Armies.

"I am God—yes, I AM. I haven't changed. . . . Return to me so I can return to you," says God-of-the-Angel-Armies.

Malachi 3:5-7

"Don't suppose for a minute that I have come to demolish the Scriptures—either God's Law or the Prophets. I'm not here to demolish but to complete. I am going to put it all together, pull it all together in a vast panorama."

Matthew 5:17

> Live the questions now. Perhaps you will then gradually, without noticing it, live along some distant day into the answer.
>
> RAINER MARIA RILKE, *LETTERS TO A YOUNG POET*

LESSON 1

1. Viktor Frankl, *Man's Search for Meaning* (Boston: Beacon Press, 1992), 87–88.
2. Norman Maclean, *A River Runs Through It* (Chicago: University of Chicago Press, 1976), 18.
3. Robert Lax, *Alley Violinist*, in *Good Poems*, ed. Garrison Keillor (New York: Penguin Press, 2003), 50.

LESSON 2

1. Harper Lee, *To Kill a Mockingbird* (New York: J.B. Lippincott, 1960), 230.
2. Louise Gluck, *A Fable*, in *The Child's Song: The Religious Abuse of Children*, by Donald Capps (Louisville, KY: John Knox, 1995), 143.
3. Anne Lamott, *Traveling Mercies: Some Thoughts on Faith* (New York: Pantheon Books, 1999), 129–131, 136.

LESSON 3

1. Edith Wharton, *The Age of Innocence* (New York: Scribners, 1993), 60–61.
2. Richard Foster, *Celebration of Discipline: The Path to Spiritual Growth* (San Francisco: Harper and Row, 1978), 80.
3. Arthur G. Gish, *Beyond the Rat Race* (New Canaan, CT: Keats, 1973), 21, quoted in Richard Foster, *Celebration of Discipline: The Path to Spiritual Growth* (San Francisco: Harper and Row, 1978), 80.

4. John Eagan, *A Traveler Toward the Dawn: The Spiritual Journal of John Eagan, S. J.* (Chicago: Loyola Press, 1990), 116–117.

5. Wendell Berry, *A Timbered Choir: The Sabbath Poems 1979–1997* (Washington, DC: Counterpoint, 1999), 5.

LESSON 4

1. Michael Yaconelli, *Messy Spirituality: God's Annoying Love for Imperfect People* (Grand Rapids, MI: Zondervan, 2002), 45, 47.

2. Henri J. M. Nouwen, *The Return of the Prodigal Son: A Story of Homecoming* (New York: Doubleday, New York, 1994), 71–72.

3. Lewis Grizzard, *The Last Bus to Albuquerque* (Marietta, GA: Longstreet Press, 1994), 194–195.

LESSON 5

1. Frederick Buechner, *The Final Beast* (San Francisco: Harper and Row, 1965), 80–83.

2. M. Scott Peck, M.D., *People of the Lie: The Hope for Healing Human Evil* (New York: Simon & Schuster, 1983), 268–269.

LESSON 6

1. John Irving, *A Prayer for Owen Meany* (New York: Ballantine, 1989), 22–23.

2. Annie Dillard, *Holy the Firm* (New York: Harper and Row, 1977), 57–59.

3. Garrison Keillor, *Lake Wobegon Days* (New York: Viking, 1985), 111–112.

LESSON 7

1. O. Henry, *The Gift of the Magi*, in *A Call to Character: A Family Treasury of Stories, Poems, Plays, Proverbs, and Fables to Guide the Development of Values for You and Your Children*, ed. Colin Greer and Herbert Kohl (New York: Harper Collins, 1995), 200–203.

LESSON 8

1. Henry David Thoreau, *Walden* (Boston: Houghton Mifflin, 1854), 25.

2. Wendell Berry, *The Hidden Wound* (San Francisco: North Point Press, 1989), 76.

3. Henri J.M. Nouwen, *In the Name of Jesus: Reflections on Christian Leadership* (New York: Crossroad, 1989), 64.

4. Richard Foster, *Celebration of Discipline: The Path to Spiritual Growth* (San Francisco: Harper and Row, 1978), 83.

5. Rhea F. Miller, "I'd Rather Have Jesus," *Baptist Hymnal* (Tennessee: Convention Press, 1991), 550.

LESSON 9

1. Garrison Keillor, *Leaving Home* (New York: Viking, 1987), 182–183.

2. Walter Wangerin Jr., *Little Lamb, Who Made Thee? A Book About Children and Parents* (Grand Rapids, MI: Zondervan, 2004), 39–46.

3. William Stafford, *One Time*, in *The Child's Song: The Religious Abuse of Children*, by Donald Capps (Louisville, KY: John Knox, 1995), 139–140.

4. Brennan Manning, *The Ragamuffin Gospel* (Sisters, OR: Multnomah, 2000), 149–150.

5. M. Basil Pennington, *Centering Prayer: Renewing an Ancient Christian Prayer Form* (Garden City, NY: Doubleday, 1980), 68–69, quoted in Brennan Manning, *The Ragamuffin Gospel* (Sisters, OR: Multnomah, 2000), 149–150.

LESSON 10

1. Wallace Stegner, *Crossing to Safety* (New York: Penguin Books, 1987), 175–176.

2. Ken Gire, *The Reflective Life: Becoming More Spiritually Sensitive to the Everyday Moments of Life* (Colorado Springs, CO: Chariot/Victor, 1998), 64–66.

3. Brennan Manning, *Abba's Child: The Cry of the Heart for Intimate Belonging* (Colorado Springs, CO: NavPress, 2002), 81–82.

4. Eugene Kennedy, *The Choice to Be Human* (New York: Doubleday, 1985), 211, quoted in Brennan Manning, *Abba's Child: The Cry of the Heart for Intimate Belonging* (Colorado Springs, CO: NavPress, 2002), 82.

GROW STRONGER IN YOUR FAITH BY WRESTLING WITH LIFE'S BIGGEST QUESTIONS.

Living the Questions in John
1-57683-834-X

On Jesus' backpack you probably would not have found a bumper sticker saying, "The Bible says it, I believe it, that settles it." The gospel of John reveals that his attitude was more like, "This is God's Word; stop and think about it, and let's talk about it."

Jesus asked more questions than he ever answered outright. Now readers and study groups can wrestle with some of these issues with this intriguing new study of the gospel of John based on *The Message*—the eye-opening translation by Eugene Peterson. Through this compelling study, readers can embrace life's questions and build a stronger faith.

Visit your local Christian bookstore,
call NavPress at 1-800-366-7788, or log on to www.navpress.com
to purchase.

To locate a Christian bookstore near you, call 1-800-991-7747.

NAVPRESS ®
BRINGING TRUTH TO LIFE
www.navpress.com